Broken Boys/ Mending Men

Recovery from Childhood Sexual Abuse

Stephen D.
Grubman-Black

 Human Services Institute
Bradenton, Florida

 **TAB BOOKS**
Blue Ridge Summit, PA

FIRST EDITION
SECOND PRINTING

© 1990 by **Stephen D. Grubman-Black**
Published by HSI and TAB Books.
TAB Books is a division of McGraw-Hill, Inc.

Library of Congress Cataloging-in-Publication Data

Grubman-Black, Stephen D.
   Broken boys/mending men : recovery from childhood sexual abuse/
by Stephen D. Grubman-Black.
     p. cm.
   ISBN 0-8306-3562-9 (pbk.)
    1. Adult child sexual abuse victims—United States—Psychology.
2. Boys—United States—Abuse of—Psychological aspects.   3. Men-
-United States—Psychology.   I. Title.
HQ72.U53G78   1990   90-33024
362.7′6—dc20   CIP

TAB Books offers software for sale. For information and a catalog, please contact TAB Software Department, Blue Ridge Summit, PA 17294-0850.

Questions regarding the content of this book should be addressed to:

Human Services Institute, Inc.
P.O. Box 14610
Bradenton, FL 34280

Acquisitions Editor: Kimberly Tabor
Development Editor: Lee Marvin Joiner, Ph.D.
Copy Editor: Pat Hammond
Cover Design: Lori E. Schlosser
Cover Photograph: Susan Riley, Harrisonburg, Virginia

Contents

In remembrance

*dedicated to the Circle of Four and to every brother whose
courage may affirm and heal us all.*

Author's Note

This book represents my coming to grips with devastating boyhood
experiences and the subsequent years of pain and anger, sadness
and fear. This book also represents portions of stories shared by
men who were also trying to understand more so they could
recover and heal more completely.

None of these men was a "case." Rather, we met and found a
deep sense of brotherhood. We shared. That experience of sharing
and caring through workshops, discussions and conversations
remains a powerful moment for us all. To have come out of hiding
and to hear us each say, "I now see I am not alone," is a gift for
all. It is in that light that this book is written.

The words are all of ours. In writing this book, I have chosen
to use the first person most of the time. I have done this so that
the reader may have a closer connection with me, the author. For
the recounting of other's experiences and recollections, I again
have chosen to use the first person singular. To use fake names or
initials is artificial; it suggests a "cover-up." I want to communicate
a realism and an honesty, and ultimately, a validity to the words
on the page. It is the "I" who says it best.

Preface

The purpose of this book is to awaken people to the realities of a grave situation. *Boys are the victims of sexual abuse*. Toward this end I have chosen to discuss and describe the interpersonal and the intrapersonal dynamics of sexual abuse. Since the perpetrator is often a man or older male who holds a significant place in the young boy's life, the boy-victim develops distorted views from a role model that could and should have been positive and constructive. The boy's views of himself are distorted, more so as he matures, because of his fears and confusions about gender identity and sexuality.

I offer this book not as a legal analysis, diagnostic tool, or treatment guide, but as a frank and uncensored discussion of a deeply troubling human problem: men need help in recovering from losses sustained from having been sexually abused as boys. This book is meant to serve as a way to educate and validate, not diagnose or prescribe. Professional workers in law, social services, counseling, psychology as well as in nursing, medicine and teaching will apply their own standards of professional responsibility to this end.

Broken Boys/ Mending Men is offered as a catalyst and as a reminder of a persistent issue confronting our society——boys are victims of sexual abuse and usually they lack support and understanding from agencies of government. Parents (and friends, spouses, partners and others significant in the adult male's life) also need to be informed and sensitized. Men, working at whatever level of mending their own "broken boy," are invited to read and consider the contents of this book. For many readers, it is an important and necessary first step toward recovery.

In this book there is a story. There is a story that some of you will recognize, sometimes for the first time, and you need to know that you are not alone. To emphasize the reality of what has happened to so many, perhaps to you yourself, a friend, a former student or relative, throughout my writing I weave the personal accounts of men who were themselves the victims of childhood sexual abuse.

Broken Boys/Mending Men is about males growing up with scars deep within them. These scars are present because these boys experienced one or more forms of sexual victimization in their childhood. Whether it is called sexual abuse or sexual assault, and regardless of degree, it was an action (or series of actions) that someone in a role of power and control (usually another male) undertook toward a boy who either didn't know it was wrong or couldn't "make it stop." In sexual victimization, the might presumes the right——here, the right of the older male to victimize sexually the young boy.

Yes, it does happen. The boy-victim is robbed. His innocence is ripped from him. And with that act, the whole world changes. One out of six males has held this secret shame, an unstated pain, an unspeakable terror that results from having been psychologically and physically hurt through an illegal (often a felony) and immoral sex act committed against him.[1]

Often, when the topic of sexual victimization of boys is raised, it is followed by expressions of disbelief. Many people do not want to admit that boys are "the other victims" of sex crimes. One of the reasons for their denial is that sexual assaults are seen as fundamentally sexual acts. And as grievous as these acts are perceived regarding female victims, our society's strong and sometimes insurmountable homophobia—fear of homosexuality—contributes to a higher and thicker wall against the truth when it comes to male victims. This, in part, explains why males are less likely to tell anyone what happened; because of their shame, confusion, and even disbelief.

Questioning the boy-victim's own sexuality diverts attention from the issue of criminality. One does not, nor should one, question the sexual orientation of a female victim of a sex crime. Yet, boys who are victimized and males who are struggling to survive and heal are confronted by accusations of latent homosexuality. The sexual orientation of the perpetrator is also doubted, so that he too is dismissed as homosexual, or a deviant, even though most child molesters are heterosexual, choosing and

---

[1] Nancy Hickey and Larry Merkel reported at a recent symposium at Temple University that 1 in 10 boys is sexually abused before the age of 15. Data from 1979, cited by Sebold (1987) suggest that the incidence is 8 percent of the population of boys. This figure is similar to the 7.3 percent of the college-age men who gave self-reports of having been sexually abused in childhood (Risin and Koss, 1987). Compare those figures to what Swift (1977) reported from survey of 20 clinicians: 33 percent of the child caseload reported sexual abuse while 19 percent of the adult caseload reported sexual abuse as young boys. It is only within the last ten years that there has been the beginnings of a supportive and informed adult world to listen to reports of childhood sexual abuse. Therefore, because of the relative recency of investigations of both the actual occurrences of sexual abuses of boys and the awakenings and realizations of men who had been sexually abused, the figure most often reported is that one in six males has been sexually abused in childhood.

exploiting their victims for reasons that may go far beyond sexual gratification alone.

This book discusses how stereotypes about men and masculinity may actually engender sexual victimization. "Real men," we are told, do and do not do certain things. The boy victims are made to feel inadequate and inferior, less like the expected image of a male. After all, why didn't he fight him off? And these whispered assessments perpetuate myths about both the perpetrator and his victims. Homophobia creates a wall, built on denial and fears. This is a theme that recurs in the personal accounts of victims.

> *MY MOTHER* seemed always to worry that I was too attractive, and I grew up knowing and fearing that I was. So when older males harassed me for my soft looks, it was one more indication that I was less than male anyway. I deserved the verbal assaults, and I guess I believed that I deserved to be attacked and treated like a mere girl. I brought it on myself, didn't I?

Why have I chosen to report the shocking details of how the abusive sexual acts occurred? Up until recently, the public has not wanted to acknowledge that boys too are victims of sex crimes. It is difficult and painful to believe. The very thought or image of a man "having sex" with a boy produces such extreme reactions that many people find it is easier and less painful to ignore or deny it. My hope is that by knowing *how sexual victimization occurs*, readers will be able to respond to this problem with greater understanding and to prevent it from happening. Perhaps one needs to be shocked by reality to counteract the systemic denial and disbelief that has existed so long. Words wield real power (ask any victim who may tell you that although few words might have been said to him, the message was clear: you tell and . . .).

Not all acts perpetrated by the adult offender on the boy are physically painful or damaging, as is oral and anal rape. Sometimes, the offender pretends to want to bring pleasure or experience to the boy. My position in writing this book is that whenever and however a boy is manipulated to become sexually involved with an older person, whether it is as a model or as a body touched or touching, fondled or fondling, exposed or exposing, it is wrong. Young boys need to know this. Parents, teachers, and therapists need to know. We all need to know so there will never again be any questions without adequate answers.

Each time I have facilitated a workshop or when I have stated the topic of my book, men have responded with stories of their own. Each one is important. There is helpful and constructive emotional release to be gained by such actions of survivors of sexual victimizations. Yet, it is not the only reason to break silence.

The offenders depended on our silence. They predicted that we would not or could not tell. The offenders depended on a conspiracy of adult silence and denial. Because the offender was an adult male with a significant role in our young lives——father, stepfather, grandfather, uncle, neighborhood or family friend, teacher, clergy——we were confused. We were hurt. We hid. In hiding, we hoped not to be discovered; not to be confronted with our own ambivalence; not to be touched and felt with our innocence invaded, our boyhood images broken, our trust destroyed.

This book is meant to encourage telling, so that feeling returns. It is meant to affirm for victims, survivors, and those others who care and want and mean to help to say that it's okay to tell. Everyone should know the extent of the hurt and pain and damage caused by the crime and the ensuing silence.

This is a book meant to touch the hearts and minds of its readers. Somehow the boy-victim is encouraged to "brave it," and survive on his own. He often struggles with the pain and shame and confusions brought on by the perpetrator. The boy-victim is a silent witness, silenced by fears and confusions, but often a boy who has changed. It requires sensitive adults to recognize these changes and their significance.

NOBODY SEEMED TO CARE anyway. I got moody and quiet, and they all figured it was a stage. I began to lose my temper and they thought that was okay too, I was starting to get tough. No matter. I didn't even understand it all. I knew that the old me was the one who was being taken advantage of, and the new me was pissed and getting positive comments for it. It was years before I started questioning why I was always so angry.

My plea is, ask again, because I know. Walk with me. Walk with all of us. There no longer is that need for isolation and loneliness. Let us work toward acknowledging and caring for victims of boyhood sexual abuse.

Acknowledgments

I wish to acknowledge, in remembrance of a past and in celebration of the present, those who shared important moments with me.

To Sheila Black Grubman, my partner in living and loving, for her faith in me, through summers in South Philadelphia, autumns in Rhode Island, winters in Buffalo, and especially for the spring, everywhere, anywhere, every one; and also for the tale of two young children waving——her from the passing car, him from the curb——at Vare Avenue, believing in Fate. YES!

To Davi Black Grubman, my child's heart, for her pride in me, our love, her spirit, and for her unique sense of timing for when and how "breaks" should occur, for the most wonderful sense of humor, for sensitivity and insight, and for respecting my commitment, preoccupation, and passion for a project that probably seemed to have possessed my very soul at times.

To the Circle of Four, whose combined strength and courage and honesty allowed me to trust my instincts and stay with the healing. I hold us within my heart and soul since we spoke and listened, wept and held in St. Louis, 1985.

To those who followed (and thereby helped guide), enlarging the circle, to each man who so honored me with the gift of trust and candor, honesty and tears, I am touched and grateful, strengthened and inspired.

To my family of friends, my brothers and sisters of choice, who have listened twice as much as you have spoken, allowing me to be nurtured and embraced, assuring me of your belief in me, sometimes even when I was uncertain, afraid, and silent, for your gentle strength, our loving relationship: Judith Anderson, Marcia Blair, Billie Conners, Sara V. Finck, Bob Germain, Ray Jones, Al Lott, Maureen McConnell, Cec Murphey, Lew Shupe, and Judy Wright each and all for hearing me through the silence, for listening and caring, and for your encouragement of my writing and your appreciation of my choices and decisions.

To those others who shared and celebrated with me the possibilities of brotherhood, especially Joe Pleck, Yevrah Ornstein, Sam Julty, David Giveans, and Franklin Abbott (for your earlier individual encouragements of my writings, especially my poetry, which have been very important); and to Charlotte Becker, Sam Becker, Lynda Heyman and Jack Becker (thank you for your caring all along, and for asking).

I also want to acknowledge the cooperation and support from the library of The University of Rhode Island, especially the Reference Department and the Inter-Library Loan Department, and from the Town of North Kingstown and the Cooperating Libraries Automated Network (CLAN) system.

To Dr. Lee Marvin Joiner, Senior Editor, Human Services Institute/TAB Books, A Division of McGraw-Hill, Inc., whose eyes heard, whose ears saw, thereby allowing this book and me to develop and to grow, accepting the challenges, guiding me in a most intriguing, sensitive, respectful and remarkable way, I offer a note of special appreciation.

Once more, to Sheila, for so many many other reasons, a topic for another book.

PART ONE

THE BROKEN BOYS

[[1]]

Image and Identity

As the fourth grade teacher peers over the papers on her desk, she wonders how her students will do on the state's standardized test. She wonders if the test will truly reveal what her children know. She might be very surprised by what Roy, now staring at the chipped paint on his desk, knows about sexual abuse. But that's not what Dad calls it.

Roy lives at home with Mom and Dad, a baby sister Lisa, and his dog, Pee Wee. Dad has a good job, with security and benefits. He is respected at work and in the community and has been described as a "family man." Dad likes to play cards with his friends once a week, and he enjoys an occasional night out with his wife. Sometimes he is seen pitching balls to his son on their front lawn. But he is never heard warning his son to keep "their little secret."

Roy and Dad seem to be so close. They can be overheard talking about places for lunch and about baseball and about other games. Just not about "that little game."

Roy might seem a little too careful now and then. Sometimes his teacher encourages him to let up on himself, assuring him that it's okay to make a mistake. At home, Roy's mother doesn't seem to notice how he sometimes cringes when his father roughhouses with Pee Wee. And she doesn't seem to notice how the father and son act in the presence of others. They are never far from each other, but they don't talk much when others are around. Yet, most of the time, everything looks pretty good, pretty normal.

Looks can be deceiving. Roy is a victim of sexual abuse. For the past fifteen months, he has been molested by his father. No one knows. And to Roy it seems like no one cares.

Roy does not remember when it all began, and he tries hard not to recall how it began. He doesn't like to think about it so, most of the time, he doesn't. He never talks about it, and he never wants to have to. It scares him. He wants to forget about it. But then Dad starts up again.

When Roy is older, he will probably feel different about himself and about others. He may avoid contact sports. He may panic if he is tackled on the football field. He may be confused in the boys' shower and he will feel ashamed. He will feel threatened too. But he won't understand much about any of that. He will understand his dad less and less, yet he will want to be like him in some ways. He's already afraid but he doesn't know it. He is angry and he doesn't know why.

Boys who are the victims of sexual abuse experience a loss of connections that in turn leads to identity problems. This loss of connections involves a loss of the spirit of youth; a loss of innocence, trust, self-esteem, and the replacement of these positive qualities with insecurity, withdrawal, isolation, and self-conscious-ness. Often, the victim's reaction to sexual abuse is termed "numbness." The big question for victims is: "Just who am I?"

The Masculine Mystique

Growing up requires a boy to watch and listen very carefully to older males. Among other things, he must learn how to think, talk and act so that he avoids being mistaken for a girl. To be labeled a girl is a curse, a handicap. It is this desire to learn and meet the expectations of the male role that is often exploited by the perpetrator.

There are many signs that indicate to a young boy that he is being accepted and respected as a male. Families, schools, churches and other socializing agencies devote considerable time and energy to teaching sex-role distinctions and reinforcing "appropriate" and "inappropriate" behaviors. However, signs of acceptance as a male are often most significant when they come from someone a boy admires, someone who is important to him. This is the older male imbued with the power of the role-model.

When a role-model's power and influence is used to coerce a boy into a relationship involving exhibition, fondling or penetration, we have met the criteria for sexual abuse. Risin and Koss (1987) have reported three criteria for sexual abuse: an age discrepancy between the child and perpetrator; the use of some form of coercion; and/or the perpetrator was a caregiver or authority figure.

The older male role-model has immense psychological leverage and when sexual abuse is involved he can effectively silence the victim. He often manipulates the boy so that he cannot distinguish between sexual abuse and closeness-attention-status. The young boy yearns for acceptance. Instead, he receives a kind of attention——often called "love" by the perpetrator——that inevitably causes confusion, shame, and disillusionment.

HE WAS STRETCHED OUT on the cot, naked. He was uncovered, so when I walked into the room he was in plain view. His body was fascinating to me. I had never seen a man completely naked before. He motioned for me to come on over, and he had me sit right next to him. He asked me if I had ever seen another guy naked. I remember that he used that word. 'Guy.' Not man. At least not right then. When I said no, he smiled and said that we weren't really that much different, did I want to see?

I was around nine or ten, and I said, sure, so he told me to take off my shirt and pants. And that was like being with a doctor because they would never tell you to take off your shorts right away, even if you were getting a shot. So, I did, and he helped me. I could feel his hands on my ribs as we rolled off my tee shirt, and he lets his hands linger on my belly and thighs as my pants slipped down. He had shifted position then, so he was seated on the cot, with his legs dangling, and my feet were across his lap. He faked struggling as he pulled off my sneakers and socks, so as my pants were removed I was pulled almost completely onto his lap. He was acting really playful and we were laughing.

And then he said, well what have we here? And he was looking down at his erect penis that was resting against my hip. I was really confused and also very fascinated. And he was talking to it and then to me, and he let me touch it. He asked me if I ever played with myself, and I said sure I did because I thought he meant playing alone. He chuckled and he asked me if I ever saw 'jit.' I didn't know what he was talking about, but he said he would show me. He said that us men had this good stuff inside us and he knew how to bring it out, and that he bet he could help me too.

He told me to show him my dick, and before I could answer, he was rolling down my shorts, so that now I was laying across his lap naked. He sat me up and he said he would show me his first, and as he held me on his lap with one arm he started to jerk off with his other hand. He was rocking and opening and closing his legs, so I was getting some ride too. As he was reaching his climax, his grip got tighter around me, and when he started spurting his stuff, he held me really close against his chest.

We repeated this little game, my uncle and me, as often as we could. He was always the man I wanted to grow up and be because he was so handsome and so popular with the ladies. And I wanted more than anything to be able to come like him. And he knew it. So he would sometimes fondle my genitals, making me feel really good, but I could never get big like him and nothing ever came out.

One day, a few months after we started this game, he asked me if I'd like to help him make the jit, and so then he was having me doing it for him. And he would have me sitting on his thighs sometimes and other times he would have me sit on his belly, and soon I was beginning to have erections, and one day he said that he would show me how we could do it together so that my first time would be with him, and wouldn't that be great because I was learning to be a man from him.

He never hurt me. Never. We did agree that I would never tell anyone. Girls, he said, wouldn't understand. And you know how he kept me quiet so I wouldn't tell other guys? He said that then all those other boys without fathers would want him to be their teacher so he couldn't spend enough time with me! And it never occurred to me to question this.

When I was thirteen, we moved away, and I missed him terribly. And he hardly ever wrote or called after that. He just kind of disappeared. I missed him so much, and I had spent so much time with him that I hardly knew how to be with boys my own age. So then I started hanging out with bigger guys, but that stuff with my uncle never happened with them. I just blocked it. Until I heard that he died a few years ago, and then I began to fall apart, not knowing why.

Sometimes boys await anxiously the first signs of sexual development to erupt. Sometimes that very natural stage is stimulated by a perpetrator in such a subtle and quiet way that the young boy does not question what is happening to him. The sexual experience may feel good. The boy does not fully understand that what is being done is wrong, nor does he foresee any of the painful consequences yet to come. Sooner or later though, he experiences destructive emotional repercussions. For example, there may be a rejection of self, a questioning of his masculinity, a feeling of malaise and insecurity.

A COUNSELOR, after hearing how I had been forced to have oral sex with a man, introduced the term "rape" as he summed up our initial meeting, and I can still remember that feeling of chill and nauseousness and then such hate and anger toward my rapist, I could just sit in the chair in the counselor's office and stare at him. Rape? Yes. Rape. Men rape women, right? So, what was that saying about me?

The boy's subsequent relationships are affected by the events instigated by a perpetrator. If the perpetrator was in a close preexisting relationship with the boy, the victims may later distrust all males because of this early violation of trust by someone significant. A boy who has been sexually victimized by an older male may grow up learning to avoid close company with men. As a "grown up" male he may dislike the masculine image he presents or that he thinks he lacks.

WHEN I WAS DATING, I was really very passive, very shy. I got a reputation as a "safe" date because I would never try anything funny. But it backfired because word got out and some of the older guys thought I was a faggot and some girls would want to date me so they could check it out. High school was a nightmare for me because I just didn't fit in. I wasn't a man.

A boy who has been sexually abused may identify with female victims of rape, constantly fearing men. This victim has learned the norms of masculinity but has come to interpret them as unacceptable because of the sexual abuse he experienced at the hands of someone who personified those standards. The result is a continuing crisis of identity.

I WAS SCARED OF MEN, their voices were so loud and there was always something that threatened me. I grew up avoiding most men, and yet I was one. For the longest time I tried to hide that fact by not being loud and trying to be gentle. But that began to stop working when I was a teenager because I got teased a lot for being so soft. I just couldn't become the kind of man who had hurt me, yet I saw where it was leading me to try to be someone so different. I was catatonic, not knowing who to be.

Some victims, like hostages, identify with the perpetrator. Pornography reinforces this reaction. Pornography legitimizes oppression, disrespect, and exploitation, expressing and dramatizing them as verbal messages and as physical acts. There is almost always the MAN and he gets the victim. In pornography, the victim often is portrayed as having wanted this horrendous treatment. Pictorial pornography usually presents caricatures as the written forms present hyperbole. The models are "equipped" or "endowed" with what is represented as desireable qualities.

I WENT TO SEE A MOVIE starring Brooke Shields called *Pretty Baby*, and I was sickened at the idea that this adult was desiring a twelve-year-old. And this was in the movies for almost anyone to watch and to laugh at. A while later it hit me that I had been younger than the girl in the story and that this guy had acted just like that Carradine character had in the movie with me. Was I too a prostitute? A female?

For the young boy who is sexually victimized, definitions of masculinity are so distorted that he grows up believing in half-truths and lies——about himself and about all men and women. As survivors, we need to reexamine the myths of masculinity that may be guiding our thoughts and attitudes. When we undertake this reexamination we often find that rigid ideas about gender roles, stereotypes based on insufficient, inadequate, inappropriate, or incorrect information, are responsible for some of our personal suffering in the aftermath of abuse. All victims should be aware that today there are new and emerging definitions of masculinity that are affirmative and positive, often based on a humanistic or feminist position.

Images of Victims

Someone once said to me after finding out I'd been abused (sexually), "We'd have never guessed just looking at you!" I hit the ceiling. It just touched a raw nerve——I think because I could swear that it used to show and that's how I got into the mess to begin with. We felt used.

I KNOW that for me the image of "used" turned around to my having been damaged goods, like a used car or a secondhand piece of clothing: not quite good enough.

Who have been the male rape victims portrayed or presented in the media? With one clear exception, Richard Crenna, most have been negative examples of current views of traditional masculinity: the boys in *Midnight Express*; the young man in *Glass Cage*; the chubby guy in *Deliverance*, for example. Jon Voight's character, in a very quick scene in *Midnight Cowboy*, is raped for his apparently unacceptable behavior with a young woman who had been used by most of the high school. This again portrays the theme that the sexual victimization of males by males is somehow "deserved" for the victim's not quite measuring up to some currently accepted image of masculinity.

Some of us succumbed to that line by giving up. Others of us fought it and worked toward perfection, fearing that we were not worthy. Either way, we have lost something. Childhood should be pleasant and warm and loving, and most of all, childhood should be safe. For the boy-victim, it never again feels safe. Either he hides to protect himself (physically, psychologically) or he strikes back. Either way, he hurts.

Having lost valuable connections, and having replaced memories with repression, the victim-survivor experiences bouts of loneliness and low self-esteem. Often the boy may feel so different, an outsider, that he hurts himself more by not being able to form satisfying interpersonal relationships.

WHO WOULD LIKE ME anyway? I knew I was different in some way, some unspeakable way. I wasn't whole. It was like I was missing an organ or a limb, damaged in a storm. And nobody wanted to be around me.

The public's images of perpetrators are not valid either. Perpetrators who commit sex crimes are rarely the wild-eyed deviants who stalk little boys. Instead, they are as familiar and close by as the same room in your home, or next door, or at a family gathering. They come in all sizes and colors, rich and poor, gay and straight, male and female.

Changing Identities

The boy who is victimized has been betrayed and a role-model for masculinity has crumbled. There is a loss of spontaneity and playfulness that could signal something has happened. No matter what the age of the first attack, the boy shows signs that something is different now. There is a fracturing of connections between the victim and the perpetrator, between his former self and the self who carries the hurt and pain, and between the victim and almost all others. Some counselors of male victims suggest that we look at photographs of the boy before the attacks or abuse and after the experiences.

FOR YEARS, I HATED TO LOOK at pictures of myself when I had been a little boy. I could never explain it. There was just something I think I disliked and was afraid to see. As an adult, I can remember one time I found a photo that had been taken of me when I was seven or eight (about two or three years after the abuse had started). I couldn't believe how unhappy and forlorn I looked. I still wasn't understanding it completely. And then, a few months ago, I brought out an old portrait of myself when I was four years old. I had this golden smile radiating from my whole face. Yes, I had once been happy and carefree. Once.

We were no more who we had been. We became something else with our name, but who was called different things. Some of us were "sweet thing." Others were "faggot," or "girl," or "sissy," or "baby." Sometimes it was "big boy" or "my little man." Most of us were referred to as special. But hardly anyone knew that the "we-had-been" was getting buried under a heap of rags and other trash.

I DON'T THINK I really knew *who* I was because I didn't know *whose* I was, though I know I knew I wasn't my own. I don't know what words can begin to describe these experiences: violated, assaulted, raped, abused, victimized . . ..

Victims identify themselves in several ways, none of which are mutually exclusive from any of the others. We have done this to survive. Some of us identified with the offender. This is especially understandable when the offender was a family member in a power and control position. Others assumed permanently the victim role, learning to placate and to avoid confrontation, usually through denial, using ourselves up over and over again. Later, as our sexuality emerged, some of us may have identified with females to the extent that we assumed a male homosexual identity—as defined by popular media or other mainstream adult beliefs.

As victims we were set up to be confused. We were spoken to and used, as parts of ourselves were labeled and related to by the offender. Some of us might have actually identified ourselves as a body part, for example, a mouth, a penis.

I NEVER FELT like inside I was really a girl, but I was made to feel that way. I was treated like an imposter, as if I was a girl in boy's clothing. I never measured up.

Some men would try to shape me up. A gym teacher, an uncle, they would try to get me interested in sports or something, just so I would fit in. But they didn't know. I was just feeling worse because nobody accepted me for me. Everybody was always trying to make me over. Nobody believed that I was man material, if you know what I mean. I was doomed to be a faggot in their minds because I didn't fit the image of man.

But nobody knew what was happening inside me, I was dying, there was no one inside me anymore. I was gone. I was just a name. For years I floated and flitted, away from most people. I was afraid. There was nobody I wanted to be.

It was just because one time I got caught putting on a girl's halter. It was innocent curiosity, I guess, I don't know. Intellectually, I figure it was just a six-year-old trying to figure things out, so I borrowed a cousin's top and was parading around the bedroom in it, looking in the mirror, playing around, when he walked in on me.

I was surprised because I thought everyone was at the beach but he came back for his cigarettes, he said. He gave me this weird look at first and then a disgusted look, saying I was wearing it wrong. I didn't understand, but I heard the word wrong. He was wearing those trunks that looked like jockey shorts, I remember, made of some shiny material. He made me get undressed. He was saying how he was gonna show me if I was a girl or a boy, and he was fondling me and making fun of me because I was squirming. He held me between his bare thighs then and was playing with my "titties." I remember he kept calling them that and I could remember thinking, "Yep, that's what I have, that's what they are."

Just then we heard the screen door slam and footsteps, and he grabbed my face and squeezed my cheeks in his hand and gestured to shut up. Then in this really vicious voice he said to get dressed fast, that he was going to take care of everything. I remember feeling really bad, guilty and wrong. I never saw him get so mad. I heard them talking, and his voice got all light and ha-ha, and all that, and then the screen door slammed and I heard the door shut.

He came back into the room and said it was going to be all right, he took care of everything, so I didn't have to worry about anybody finding out. And I was relieved, I was really grateful to this bozo who was my sister's boyfriend. I was safe, my secret was going to be safe with him.

He changed again, this time he was attentive and friendly, telling me it was okay by him if I wanted to wear girl's clothes. And he got naked then and said to go ahead and see. He made me put back on the halter top and he made me look at him so I could see I made him excited. He made me touch him there. And again, and then he said my secret was gonna be safe with him. He made it all seem okay that summer, but always I felt that I was wrong except with him and that I had to keep the secrets.

It is understandable that a sexually victimized boy would become confused and that he may remain confused and insecure about his identity. The boy is initiated into behaviors he may learn to accept as normal, based on the status of the perpetrator in his life, e.g., father, uncle, teacher, or pastor. The boy learns to accept victimization in terms of how he is identified by the perpetrator ("good buddy," "son," "faggot anyway") and how strongly he identifies with the perpetrator.

I DIDN'T KNOW WHAT I was supposed to be. At fourteen I was made to have oral sex. But it was really confusing. My uncle, who was also my godfather, was always pretty close, and nobody ever thought anything because we really got along and he was my godfather. We went away on a camping trip. That's when it happened.

But it started out with him admiring me and how big I was getting, and teasing me about how big I really was, and I really trusted him so it was going to be easy to ask him about sex and girls I figured. My father was really stand-offish, and he never told me anything. We got to this spot in this incredible place that was so quiet and beautiful. He had rented a cabin on the lake and there was a kind of a waterfall or rushing water nearby too. He had bought me everything for the trip, all my supplies, and I was in heaven.

It was the middle of the afternoon and he said we could cool off and wash off at the same time. He said we could strip and just bring a towel so we could dry off afterward. I was real shy so I wrapped my towel around my waist, but he didn't.

It was funny but he would always put an arm around me when we'd be walking or something, and he was doing this now, but it was feeling different. He must have known that because he said to relax and I got used to it as we trekked to the place where the stream with the kind of waterfall was. It was pretty far to walk in bare feet, and I guess I was starting to limp around. We stopped and he made me lean against a tree and said he's checking to see I'm okay. He lifted my leg on his thigh and my towel got loose, but he said never mind and he wiped my foot. When he took the other one he bent over and got real close to my middle.

I couldn't help it and I was getting a hard-on and he says it's fine because it's natural. We're not moving then and he's staring. He says that he was going to wait till he taught me to drive but it's okay now so he wants to show me something, and he takes it in his mouth and before I could say anything I explode in his mouth. He says I was good, and I think I know what he means, but I'm not sure.

We get to the water and he and I cool off with the water cupped in our hands. Then I hear him telling me to look, and he shows me his big hard-on. He says let's take care of things and he says, 'Do I want to do him?' I'm real scared now, but he doesn't make me do anything.

After a while we spread out our towels and lay down, me on my stomach and him on his side facing me. He tells me that what he did was real special and that I gave him my seed which was really special too. He tells me some other stuff I don't remember but it's like I'm getting hypnotized. I feel his hand on my butt and he reaches down between my legs to get a feel. I'm hard again and he says I should give it space so I turn over but away from him so he won't see.

He's still talking about nature and natural and all that stuff and I can feel him moving. He's up on his feet and he says it's time to head back. It's like I'm totally out of it now, like he's splashed cold water on me as I slept. I don't understand. It was so sudden, this change. But I get up, he helps me by pulling me up, and we walk back to the cabin, his arm on my shoulder and now I'm feeling okay again, like it's all gonna be all right, that this is special, that he and I are special.

He asks me a couple of more times over the week to do him, and I keep saying no. But I feel really bad. He looks so sad. And he never did me again even though he would make a comment about that nice and special time we had. I really wanted it though, and I think he knew it.

The last evening out there he said we should have a special time, and I know he saw me get all excited in my crotch. We drove about an hour to this restaurant and he even let me take a couple of sips of his beers. On the way home he drove with his hand rubbing the back of my neck and then moved it down to my thigh, rubbing almost up to my hard-on. He asked me to put my hand on his leg like that, which I did.

We were real cozy in the car that way and he was really nice like he always was to me.

We got to the cabin, but we sat in the car for a while because, he said, this was such a special night for him and he didn't want it to end. He was crying, and I didn't know what to say. I never saw a man cry before, but I knew he was no kind of faggot or anything. He said for me to pull down my pants, that he wanted to make me feel special one more time before we had to leave, and I nearly ripped them to get them down fast enough. He chuckled then, and said no woman would ever make me feel as good and he started on me.

Then he stopped, and said he was getting uncomfortable because he didn't have enough room for his grand thing, so he shifted and moved meanwhile pulling his pants and shorts down too. He asked me to just hold it a little and would I kiss it, which I did. Then he finished me off.

We sat there then for a long time. I never did do him, but I did let him do his special thing for me for a couple of years. Every once in a while he would ask me but I would only maybe touch it or maybe kiss it and once I did let him put it in my mouth. But that's all. I'm not a queer. Him neither really because I was the only one and we never did anything else.

It is not my purpose to try to analyze the mind of the offender. I have no tolerance for the perpetrators of the crime. My concern is for the victims and the survivors. Those of us who were abused may now recognize how the lines and boundaries between boy and offender have been moved, stretched or erased. We were children whose rights and needs were denied. We were required to meet someone else's definition us and of him. We were unable to escape the dream that was not of our making or choice. Whatever we sought, for whatever we needed, we were met with one fixated response. I needed to be held and hugged, not fondled or aroused. We needed companionship and guidance, not sexual initiation. For many of us, there was emptiness in our lives. The offender chose to fill his own emptiness, his own needs, leaving us to feel even more barren.

A child needs childhood. We were not supposed to give it up to someone who often should have served as our protector or parent. That person took something from us, and for many survivors, it has taken a long time to see that we have an identity way beyond that of victim. Recovery is a process to help us move from one role to the other.

It may be helpful and beneficial for us to take a few moments to compare imagery and associations with the two words: victim and survivor. With which word does each of us identify?

⟦ 2 ⟧

CHAPTER

Feelings
and Other Confusions

Confusion and feelings of fear, shame and regret are rampant among sexually victimized boys. Tragically, being a child-victim offered opportunities to feel good, to feel admired, loved, and wanted. Yet the existence, or even fulfillment, of a lonely child's need for love, approval, and nurturance neither mitigates the liability of the sex criminal nor inculpates the child-victim. The adult manipulated a young boy's emotional needs, misusing his own role in that boy's life.

Most of us who have survived sexual victimization are "good boys." Either we try harder or we try to be perfect. We often occupy positions in helping professions and we take on many additional responsibilities in life. We are "good boys," but once we thought of ourselves as "bad boys." The purpose of this chapter is to examine this good boy/bad boy dichotomy, the feelings and other confusions which stem from it, and to explore alternative views of self.

The movies of the old west that were popular in the fifties and sixties were filled with examples of the "good men" and the "baddies," shown vividly through clothing color (the baddies always wore dark colors) and personal appearance (the good men always were clean-shaven and their hair never seemed out of place). We learned from these images. As young boys, we and others saw us as good. Some of us, perhaps as a reflection of needs arising from a dysfunctional family, were forced to strive for even greater perfection.

I WAS A GOOD BOY. I did everything I was told. I ate all my vegetables. I even finished them first before I would start on my meat. I spent years trying not to be bad. I knew deep down inside that I must have been bad, that I had done something really wrong. I did not understand what that was, but I just knew I was bad. I never saw it as *it* was bad or *he* was bad. It always fell on me, that I was the one, it was my fault. So I tried for the longest time trying to avoid a feeling or a spirit of being bad without understanding or knowing what any of it was all about.

Good boys think of others. They help people. They are not selfish. Good boys are obedient. I wrote a poem, entitled *Poses*:

sit
be still
don't say anything
don't talk to anyone
look straight ahead and walk
be a good boy
listen to me
be nice
stay
don't go
that's not nice
where are you going
you must be home now
look when i speak
don't be fresh
you'll see
no.

> not words of wisdom these
> but orders barked
> they worked their way
> till they lost meaning
> and the mannequin moved

One of the most helpful books I read was Alice Miller's *Drama of the Gifted Child*. She opened my eyes to the kinds of twisted paths I had been forced to take in order to try to satisfy a parent who was insatiable and narcissistic, self-center-ed and selfish. Nothing I was ever to do would have been good enough, but I had tried for so long, losing myself more and more. As a victim of sexual victimization, I had been forced to neglect me because she was so busy worrying and obsessing about her and her own needs and comforts. I was neglected and I was a victim.

What struck me too is how much of me had been used by lots of other people who saw that I really wanted to be a good guy and who would tap into that reservoir. Sure, everyone could depend on me. Sure, I would do anything . . . for a price. I paid very heavily. I was heading for a physical and emotional breakdown in my early thirties and I had nothing to show for it. Most of my relationships were based on what I could do for others. I had few good friends. I was too busy "ministering" to everyone else. I was the ultimate good guy, the knight in shining armor, the messiah.

Good Boy/Bad Boy?

When the rules change quickly, and when you're not even sure what the rules are supposed to be, what's right and what's wrong? But knowing the difference between right and wrong is not, and never was, the responsibility of a victim of crime. That is the offender's responsibility. The offender knows that his sexual conduct is immoral and illegal. The child-victim, on the other hand, may not know until it is too late, as when penetration occurs. Instead of dwelling on what's right or wrong, he is confused and frightened because someone he trusts is betraying him.

I WAS A VERY GOOD BOY, in fact I was the best little boy there was. I was polite, helpful, smart, studious, cooperative, quiet. But all that got twisted somehow and thrown back in my face by the offender. He made it sound like that's why I was in such trouble now. But I still tried to be good. I even tried harder. I felt wrong. Now I know I wasn't. I was being wronged. But then I felt like I should have been better at being a normal boy, so I tried hard to do that, be the best normal boy in the whole world.

It's odd, but I think I'm both good and bad, even now. It didn't matter what I did, I guess, because it kept happening. So it's the same now. I can do a good job but it doesn't last. It's like I can't take it, so then I screw up, and I feel better. I just don't know. I'll say, yeah sure I'll do it, but something happens and I don't or I do it wrong.

Back then, before he got started with me, I was really good. But it got really strange. I remember everybody getting mad at me because I wouldn't eat, and they kept saying I was wasting food and all that. I couldn't tell them. I couldn't say that lots of food made me want to puke, and I couldn't stand anything that would burn my throat. It was awful. I didn't understand it either. I just knew I was gonna puke. I ended up with tonsillitis and everybody thought that was my problem, but it wasn't. They said I was a bad eater. Not him. Now I still go through times when I will stuff my mouth with food for months and then I go on these strict diets. And there's still some food I will not eat. And I always got bad sore throats. Even now.

Did we try to be good so people would like us or so we would not be the object of the perpetrator again? As young boys, trying to emerge from the victim role, we may have tried to do or be the opposite of what we thought placed us in jeopardy. On the other hand, we may have learned to pursue the "good" track to prevent worse things from happening, thereby becoming the rescuers we longed for. We tried to be good, not always understanding why.

Some of us gave up and became (often to ourselves) "bad." Especially in adolescence, we might have decided to give up trying to be the "good boy." It did not seem to be working out anyway.

I HAD THIS REALLY TOUGH, hard-ass gym teacher in junior high. He took an instant dislike to me, so no matter what I did or tried, he was on my case. He would yell and insult me. Finally one day I let him have it. I yelled back. He was just getting too much for me. He sent me to the office, and I almost got suspended.

Well, after that, there was no use. It didn't matter. But I was getting support from the other guys in my class, so I got better, or I guess it was worse, at giving this teacher a hard time. It was easier in gym class to do that. Now I look back at that whole scene and I wonder if my manner offended him or if he was an offender. I don't know, but I have my suspicions.

A lot of our energies were misdirected; we were trying to be the "best," and, it seems, no matter how hard we tried or what we did, it backfired. Often, this followed us into adulthood, as we worked to be someone else's "best."

Sexuality

Confronting their early sexuality is a key problem for many males who struggle with surviving and healing. For many survivors of sexual victimization, sexuality is not an easy or comfortable topic to think or talk about. The discomfort often stems from feelings of shame, guilt and embarrassment, some of which developed early but only surfaced much later in the victim's life.

SHE "TOOK ADVANTAGE" of me. That's the way I began to see it. And then I would have trouble with women because I felt like such a wimp.

Early sexuality issues for victims of boyhood sexual abuse are further complicated by homophobia since most perpetrators are male. There remains in our society a very deep fear of homosexuality. This homophobia is so strong that even the possibility that one's son is attracted by, or attractive to, other males sends shivers, panic, and dread through parents and even professionals.

As products of this society, we who have begun to recognize and acknowledge our past sexual victimizations are also devastated by our own feelings of homophobia. If the perpetrator was male, we struggle with the ambivalence——the confused thoughts and feelings——surrounding having been selected, aroused, and pleasured by a male.

HOW COULD I have been turned on by another male? He made me feel good. But I later learned that was wrong. So I chose to forget.

For many boys who are victims of sexual abuse, the attention by an older male was enjoyed and perhaps even invited at times. The attention that was accompanied by physical closeness, touching, fondling, and even more direct sexual contacts was accepted because it was meeting a basic human need for closeness and warmth. Over and over, I am impressed by the numbers of us who, as young boys, ached for attention and love, protection and guidance, and when we found someone (or, more accurately, when he found us), we were open, needy, vulnerable . . . and ready to be victimized.

I RECALL READING a novel about a boy who was kidnapped and raped by a man. As the story unfolded, the reader was told of a special bond that was occurring between the two main characters. So, by the end of the book, the boy lied about the identity of his perpetrator. He lied to protect him. And I think he also lied to protect himself. Isn't there a line from a song that goes something like this? "How could something that feels so good be so wrong?"

It is often the double-bind of budding feelings of sexuality and the security of the older male's attention that caused confusion in later life, long after the victimization has ended.

I WAS ONCE WARNED—too late and too little information—about child molesters. Well, sort of. I think what I was really being warned about was homosexuals. I was about fourteen then, and I was a good-looking kid. My mother told me that I should be careful. There were men who would do stuff to me and it would make me feel good. But I should stay away from them. Seriously, that's all I was told.

And I was really confused, but I didn't know exactly why. You see, I had been sexually molested when I was about six, and I didn't know that's what it was, so I just kind of forgot about it. But now I was thinking maybe I wanted to meet one of those men. To feel good again. But I didn't think about it as a repeat. Just that I found out some mystery of growing up and I wanted to know more.

Often victims are denied opportunities for self-understanding and self-acceptance. Secrets, lies, half-truths are made in darkness. Too often, adults maintain the silence, fearing the very nature of sexuality. This continues the disempowerment of the boy-victim by keeping him ignorant or ill-informed.

I CAN RECALL that when I first started to ejaculate, I was confused and scared. It was the intensity of the feeling. Such pleasure. I was afraid and ashamed though, so I would try to stop. And when that didn't work, I would hide. I mean,

I would wrap my penis all up so I would be trying to hide it and reduce the pleasurable sensations.

It wasn't until years later, when I realized I had been sexually abused as a boy, that I figured I was trying to deal with all that stuff.

"All that stuff" is the fulcrum of the issues. Indeed, "all that stuff" has guided me in the recording and in the writing of this book. We can see that the adult survivor of sexual victimizations in childhood is confused and hurt. He had been betrayed. He lost someone's trust. He was physically hurt. He ended up abandoned. Yet, we also need to recognize confusions, uncertainties, and dangers that emerged from these premature and therefore misunderstood sexual experiences.

The burdens of denial, forgiveness, and secrecy are indeed crushing and suffocating for the boy-victim. As boys, we were put off balance many times, not knowing or understanding how to react to our own feelings, yet feeling responsible for someone else's. We grew up too fast. A ten-year-old is not supposed to be worried or concerned about "taking care" of someone else's physical needs. A seven-year-old boy is not physically or emotionally prepared to be a "surrogate" sexual partner for one of his parents. A fifteen-year-old should not feel that his only escape from a situation that is taking advantage of his physical excitement exists in drugs, self-inflicted injury or prostitution.

The offender has convinced himself and his victims that it is all okay. And when we were feeling "okay" or "good," it reinforced the message. But one day—and it is precisely the point I wish to make for all of us—we wake up and realize that we were victims. The fallout from that awakening is damaging.

I refuse to orgasm to ejaculation.
I can't function.
I'm afraid I'm bisexual.

I figured I was gay, but I didn't want to be, so I'm nothing.
I have to be in control. All the time.
I can't come, when I'm with somebody.
I was a prostitute.
I'm afraid.

Fears

Why are so many of us afraid? What do we fear? Who is it we fear? Some of us are afraid of discovery. We fear someone discovering something about us that is "wrong" or "bad" or "dirty." We fear making discoveries about ourselves, about our human frailties, in essence, fearing discovery of our basic humanness. "What if I actually enjoyed it? Even a little. Even some of the time." We fear repercussions or retribution, punishment and misunderstandings. We fear opening up and letting go of some of the memories and thoughts and feelings we hid with and hid from for so long. Whom we have feared, besides the offenders and those who resembled them, has been ourselves.

I FELT GOOD when we were together. He showered me with gifts and attention. And he knew how to get both of us going.

I FOUGHT HIM at first. But he excited me. And soon I was hooked.

IT WAS LIKE I was out in the cold, with ice-cold rain soaking me. And he was the warmth and the comfort from the storm. He would make me want to do things with him. Not like he was forcing me. I just felt so good inside and it just seemed a natural thing to do. I still don't know. I was a little boy when it started. I don't know. Sometimes even now I will think about it, fantasize. Then I feel so guilty.

There are often remnants of childhood feelings, especially shame, guilt, and embarrassment, which persist into adulthood. During adulthood these feelings become even more troubling as the adult becomes more aware of their possible meaning.

Even if the adult coerced him, he may have felt some wave of pleasure. If he accepted gifts for favors, or if he yielded to the moment's excitement or the adult's strength or cunning, the boy-victim is blamed. He is manipulated, if not coerced, to assume some of the responsibility, some of the guilt. At some point (then, later, now), he recognizes that it was wrong. He was part of the "it." He still remembers it, especially when he awakens to the whole experience, and he feels worse. He feels guilty. Part of that guilt seems to be self-imposed, yet it is not. He was made to feel guilty so that the adult could feel vindicated.

Some of us also have been told that if we fantasize about something, it means that we want it. In the arena of sexuality, however, it is not so simple. First, in a fantasy, the one who holds the fantasy, i.e., the daydreamer, is in control. He can and may change any part or moment he wishes to. Second, the adult whose fantasy may be partially based in a childhood experience has the advantage over the child by fully understanding that it is a fantasy. We do not have to pursue it now. The boy-victim, on the other hand, had no right of informed choice.

The issue of *homophobia* again arises as the victim at some point connects his experiences with what society has labelled homosexual. The act may become his label. He is confused and guilty, choosing perhaps to bury his feelings only to have them reemerge later in adulthood. We are afraid of ourselves, blaming the boy we had been, fearing that it was the boy who made us do it, who made us who we are today.

Fears are forever (for some).

The sexually victimized boy often feels intense fear of his oppressor. Not knowing what else to do about it, he may assume a mask. Attempting to hide does not help, although it may work for a while. The fears remain and usually grow beyond the recognition or understanding of the survivor.

A FEW YEARS AGO I was in a situation with a friend of mine, also a survivor of sexual abuse, where he was needing a lot of comforting. He had been getting upset and was feeling very scared and down. I opened my arms and held him close against me, and we kind of rocked, and his tears started flowing and I was feeling very very close to him. We stayed this way for a few moments, and I was soothing him, stroking his forehead and telling him it was going to be okay, when these words popped out of my mouth: "It's okay, I'm not gonna hurt you." And he popped up and said why did I say *that*?

I didn't even realize what I had said. And as we continued to talk, I remembered a scene that had been recreated. I realized that I had never put myself in a situation where I was physically close to anyone, not even to comfort a person, especially another man. I remembered that the man who molested me had started out by comforting me.

I had been very upset and was crying. He had brought me to a private spot and as he closed in on me. I calmed down and was still seeking his attention and comfort. He began to fondle me more and more, and as he continued to expose us both—I can still, if I let myself—feel his warm chest, he said, "It's okay, I'm not gonna hurt you." I can hear him.

Since then I had been so afraid of physical closeness. And I realize I had been afraid of emotional closeness too. I suspected deep down that people had ulterior motives and I feared that I too was guilty.

When we do not remember or understand the source of our fears, we constantly sense danger. We react inappropriately or aversively to situations that are benign. Eventually, we lose trust and regard for ourselves and our instincts.

WHENEVER I VISIT a new place, like a museum or a concert hall or a theater or even a strange home, I always check out the exits. I have to know how to get out before I am comfortable because I am deathly afraid of being trapped and not knowing how to save myself.

When I was a boy, I was in a new and strange place, and I woke up in the middle of the night not knowing where I was or what to do. I got up out of the bed and wandered around in the dark till I was found by the man of the house who sodomized me. He made sure I never had a night light and that the hall light was turned off, and I would get up to go to the bathroom and always be walking right into him.

I felt trapped in that place. So now I am still afraid of not knowing how to get out of a place, even a supermarket or restaurant, and I need lights. I just remembered too that elevators and airplanes are fearsome for me, but I just figure I could find the escape door on the roof of an elevator and I could jump out of a plane.

The extent to which we go to attempt to survive is certainly impressive, yet the emotional energy consumed is almost too great.

I FEAR BOTH failure and success. Crazy, huh? I am afraid of being wrong but I am also afraid to do too well because then I'll be noticed.

I was singled out in camp because I did all my chores so well so I got to have special privileges. I was also afraid to slip up because of this honor. I tried so hard to be careful and right, and this one counselor knew that. So, he worked on both fears, I suppose. I was expected to do even more and there was a responsibility attached. I was afraid to mess up so I used all my special privilege time to get even better.

After a while, he was manipulating me so I would feel inferior and he started to move in on me. I would cry out of frustration and he would comfort me, holding me against him at first. And I can still hear him say as he was making his moves to not be afraid. "Don't be afraid."

Over that summer, I lost confidence and my innocence. The irony was that the camp director encouraged my parents to send me back there next year because I had made such progress in maturity, according to counselors' reports. I refused to go, and they sent me to another summer camp the next years where they reported I moped and refused to cooperate.

The signs were there. Why didn't others pick up on the changes of the boy and pursue them? Perhaps because the adult too is afraid.

THE FEAR I HAD when I was growing up as a teenager is that it would show and that the older guys would know and then they would want to do it. I was petrified it still showed. I became a zombie at first and then I learned to fight, so I would protect myself. But the fears of being overtaken followed me.

I am afraid of attention because I want always to be in the background, to go unnoticed. That's what must have gotten me in trouble in the beginning. I was too obvious, I guess. So I work at just being plain.

As males, we need assurance that it is okay to be afraid. Fear is a reality, and when we are able to understand our fears and their origins, it is liberating.

"I didn't trust touch."

If, as in the more traditional views of males and females, it is accepted that one gender must be the dominant one, the aggressor, then boys who have been sexually victimized have also lost self-esteem. Boy-victims of female offenders also have to deal with confused and ambivalent feelings about their early sexuality because they have violated traditional dominance-related roles and expectations for males. As grown-ups, they continue to be confused and constrained by roles and responsibilities which may differ from those forced on them earlier.

I WAS HAVING these strong erotic feelings about boys in ninth grade with me, but at home my mother was literally attacking me for sex. I hated it and I was very confused. It took me years after that to acknowledge my sexuality and my sexual preference. It took too long and I have a failed marriage and a lot of hate and anger too.

The confusions surrounding sexuality are great. Often, we have asked of ourselves, "Who are we *really*?" only to be answered with labels written by the damaging events of our pasts.

EVERY TOUCH is sexual to me. I think that I was ruined because I misinterpret anyone who touches me or even flatters me, like if I'm wearing something nice, I figure that person wants only one thing from me, and that's sex. I am hungry for touch, but I am so afraid, so threatened by the idea. I miss out on a lot, I know, but the risks scare me so.

A few years ago, I had this really unique experience. I think that it was because I was feeling very safe. It happened at a men's conference. The whole conference had been a wonderful experience for me. I met lots of people (mostly men) who were committed to a world that would be just for all people regardless of gender, race, age, sexual preference, or physical appearance. Everyone was so gentle and so caring and friendly, so I was feeling affirmed and supported. I did say it was a wonderful experience, didn't I!

Anyway, there was this spirituality session where many of the participants met on the beautiful grounds of Tufts University on a warm and sunlit morning and we sang and danced and moved together in this beautiful circle of love. Then the leader of the ceremony had us pair off with someone near us, and since I didn't know anyone I figured that I would just kind of move to the side, but the guys next to me (who seemed to have been together) moved closer to me and we joined hands and sat together. Then the leader told us to close our eyes and to let our hands touch our partner.

At first it was the three of us awkwardly trying, but there was something within me that I felt become released and I reached for one of them and he let go of his partner, who then kept his hand on each of us without interfering, and this other guy and I held and hugged each other on the grass under the June sky. It was absolutely one of the most beautiful experiences I had had up to that point in my life, and it was so meaningful because I didn't fear nor did I regret. I was relaxed and accepting, and it was one of the first times in my life that I didn't worry about my sexuality or about sex. This was sensual. It was loving and supportive. I also believe that my partners had been extremely sensitive with me. They felt and they followed my instincts, I believe.

I was 36 years old when that happened. I had been deprived and that deprivation had scared and threatened me so, I did not trust touch because I believed it was "wrong" by which I mean it was taboo or sexual.

We have the potential—we have the right—to be sexual beings. We need to understand that regardless of the sensations and feelings associated with our early victimizations, these experiences did not define our sexuality. Nor did they define or

describe our sexual preferences. We should never permit them to
define who we are now.

It's Everybody's Shame

Often the victim is shamed into thinking that he is "good
enough" to use sexually, but not to respect, so he accepts the
shame.

> *I WAS CAUGHT*. I mean, that's how I felt. This crazy guy
> corners me in a hospital. I'm waiting in one of those big
> rooms where there are lots of examining tables, separated by
> curtains, and in he walks. I was around seven, and I think he
> must be a doctor (he was wearing a white outfit). Anyway he's
> exposed himself to me and he's got me out of the hospital
> gown and rubbing himself against me, and all of a sudden, the
> curtain is torn open, gliding noisily on its rings across the bar,
> and my mother yells what are you doing! And this guy, without
> turning around, tells her to wait outside, which she does, and
> he runs out the other side.
>
> So there I am, scared and confused. Another guy comes
> in, also in white, and she follows after him and demands to
> know where the first doctor is. He shrugs and tells her to go
> out, and he finishes examining me. Afterward, I'm really quiet,
> and she keeps asking what was going on in there, and I really
> don't know, so I just clam up and she keeps ranting till I tune
> her out but I keep thinking that what I did in there was wrong.

We acquired and maintained a shameful attitude, blaming
ourselves for what had happened to us. This is understandable
when we also consider how little has been spoken about sexual
victimization of boys and how little support and understanding has
been available. In that light, it's everybody's shame.

WHEN I STARTED to realize I had been sexually abused as a child, I was already an adult. And I can remember over and over again feeling like I was confessing something. The guilt and the shame were overwhelming. I am still ashamed to tell it. I blame myself a little even now.

Sometimes I panic when I'm feeling too good, like when I'm enjoying my sexuality. Even now, as an adult male, after counseling and group work. Sure, I'm better for it, but still there's this voice that once in a while still hisses, "Oooo, lookit what you're doin'! And you're ENJOYING it too!" That's the part that brings guilt and shame to me. It's when my sex partner is being so extra kind and wonderful to me, bringing me to a beautiful level, and it's like I open my eyes and there in the shadows is some little bastard wagging his finger and saying I ought to be ashamed of myself. I skip a heart beat then and sometimes I even have tried to get away, which usually creates a struggle and that sometimes leads to more of a fantasy being played out too.

To get caught is to admit weakness, defeat, and that I must have really wanted it anyway. So, pleasure and humiliation come out, and I am so ashamed of myself. I sometimes even repeat this little head game with the same person, only they don't know about it. I wouldn't tell. I'm too ashamed.

Regrets

There are many things to regret for survivors of sexual victimization. For some, the regret is for not having had a normal childhood or a normal household. Regrets may center around a certain issue such as time, a conversation, or an opportunity to disclose. The issue of regret is far-reaching.

I'VE REGRETTED that I never had the chance to challenge him, to face him in a court of law and accuse him of the heinous crimes he committed against me.

THE THING THAT I REGRET most of all is that I've been so messed up sexually all this time so that I have hardly ever allowed myself to enjoy sex. I'm always so in need of control.

Feelings of regret are normal. It is what we do with feelings of regret that counts. When they drive us and hold us down, it is time to try to move on. We all deserve to live a life filled with self-acceptance, love, respect, and trust. As we move and struggle toward healing and recovery, we learn to accept that to feel good emotionally, socially, spiritually, and physically is what indeed we deserve in every way, everyday.

AIDS: New fears for old times.

A very sad and frightening fact is that thousands of children contract sexually transmitted diseases (STD's). The only way that could have happened, other than through blood transfusion or by birth, is by having had some form of sexual intercourse. Bodies and souls, physical and emotional health, outside and inside, all victims have sustained risks. The long-term effects of these risks may be very long indeed.

I WAS ORALLY RAPED when I was about five-and-a-half years old. He took me off to a secluded spot, which I readily agreed to go to because I knew and trusted him so well. The pain, the way he changed toward me right after, his anger, disgust, and bullying, and the confusion and fear I had, so terrified me that I became disassociated from myself.

I immediately "forgot" what had happened, and remained unconscious of it and him for a good many years. But I do remember that around that time, I missed a lot of school because I came down with a lot of illnesses. One of the illnesses I had was hepatitis. It took a long time for me to get over it. Well, this is crazy but when I started hearing about AIDS and different strains of hepatitis I got really upset. What if he gave me AIDS? I mean, I know that's impossible because my rape occurred in 1951 or so, and AIDS wasn't around. But you know, I started thinking what if he had given me some other sexually transmitted disease and no one knew it then and they just gave me antibiotics for the hepatitis. Or what if they knew! Anyway, I get scared not only for myself but for the victims of sexual assaults now.

This is a dreadful predicament for anyone to be forced to face. His nightmares may be true. His night terrors may be real.

A recent headline in a newspaper (*The Providence Journal-Bulletin*, June 9, 1989) read: "Victims of childhood rape more likely to be infected with AIDS later - study." The researchers, Sally Zierler and Kenneth Mayer, from Brown University, suggested that the feelings of guilt, sexual acting out, and self-destructive behaviors may contribute to a former victim's becoming infected with AIDS later in life. So, this appears to be a twist on the concerns we may have about relationships between STD's and childhood sexual victimization. We not only need to be concerned about immediate medical issues but we also need to be concerned about the range of by-products of the assaults.

Victims need to be recognized, supported, helped, and accepted. Since we know that a complexity of issues has prevented early identification, assessment and treatment, perhaps this information about the immediate and long-term concerns regarding STD's will help.

Abandonment

I can remember when someone was starting to teach me to swim. He suggested that floating on my back would be a good way to begin. So, with promises extracted from him, I lay in the water, with him at my side, and tried to float. But he moved away and I splashed and then sank until he grabbed me from the water, admonishing me for having been too rigid and tense. But inside my head I kept asking, "Why did you leave me?"

Eventually, the perpetrator will abandon the victim, physically or psychologically, or both. For the victim, abandonment is a terrifying possibility. Our fear was multiplied because we were made to feel that it was up to us, whether he stayed or whether he left. We were made to feel afraid of losing someone, and if we did, we blamed ourselves or we were blamed by someone else.

When the man who raped me stopped visiting my mother, she never questioned why he never came back except to ask me again and again what I had said to make him look and act so mad when he and I returned from the stables. I had failed not one, but two.

The threat of abandonment had probably always been implicit since a perpetrator knows that sexual acts with a boy are immoral and illegal and must eventually cease. Invariably, if a positive role-model relationship has been established with the boy, the perpetrator will use the threat of this abandonment as a means of control or insurance.

If you tell, they won't let us be together.
If they find out, they won't let me be with you.
Nobody else understands you like I do.

Sometimes the perpetrator will threaten to sabotage or destroy an important relationship or harm the boy's parents.

If you tell, it'll kill your mother.
If you tell, I'll hurt your parents, and then nobody will be around to take care of you.

The perpetrator is an archetype of dysfunctional male-male relationships. Even when we grew up and away from the perpetrator, his mark remained on us.

AS AN ADULT, surviving the insanity of previous assaults against myself, I still carried a heavy fear of being abandoned. On the one hand, I knew that to be abandoned would leave me more alone and more isolated than ever before. And that sense of loneliness follows me to this day. Then again, the fear of being abandoned is so great that often I would acquiesce. And that sense of fear is even more hurtful and it has turned out to be even more dangerous.

I never quite knew how to say no. I was afraid to refuse or to assert myself because then nobody would like me. So many of my relationships were based on conditional acceptance. Over and over, I would find myself in relationships that were very destructive, and none of them were sexual. They were just as bad as the original abuses though.

In each case I sought to make things right by making certain the other person was satisfied or happy. The original loss of my self through early sexual victimization continued.

The man who did it to me had promised to return, and he never did. He had used me . . . and bought my silence with promises afterward that we would get together lots of times and he would be nicer to me. So I looked forward to feeling better and I waited for him to return, but he never ever came back. Weeks went by, and no word came. And I waited.

After a while I think I figured that I must have done or said something wrong to him, and he was mad at me, so he was punishing me. Couple that childhood perception with the feeling that I had been abandoned by other caregivers and that's how I ended up with him. So I feared that if only I had done this or that, he would not have stayed away, leaving me alone.

Then again, I would enter relationships where there never was a very fair balance. I would do practically anything in order to keep the person with me. I can remember lots of instances when I would submerge my wants and needs in order to have someone stay with me, and often I would be hurt. I can vaguely recall pleading with my perpetrator so that it wouldn't be so painful and scary, promising him I'd be good. And still he left me.

The lesson I seemed to have learned from all this is that I should have done even more. And in later situations, I played this out. I was abandoned so I figured I had one choice in relationships: Don't get close. Beat them to the punch. Leave first. And so that's what I do. I run first because the pain of rejection and abandonment is much too much to handle. It hurts too much.

Often, we do not know that these responses to others, whether in personal, professional, or casual relationships, are prompted by our early experiences of having been abandoned.

I AM NUTS when it comes to being abandoned. I am always early to pick up my child and I am always worrying that she'll be waiting for me.

There remains inside me this little boy who still feels betrayed and abandoned by the adult, so now I have these feelings but they've generalized to most people. For me, the easy way to deal with this is to most of the time not open and get close.

Whenever I hear that someone I feel close to is moving, or is dying, or is ill, or is late, or if that person doesn't call me back soon enough or write back to me soon enough, or whatever, I get scared. I feel abandoned, and then I withdraw. It's awful because I end up giving conflicting messages to people: I need you, I want you, and it has to be now and always and forever, BUT if for any reason you don't live up to my needs and expectations, just forget it. I don't want to bother with you. Good-bye. That way I get to say good-bye first.

Male victims of sexual abuse and assault make personal compromises in order to avoid a repeat of their earlier rejection and abandonment. For example, we may remain in psychologically unhealthy or physically dangerous relationships long after we should have left them. On the other hand, we might have left a relationship prematurely, after the initial "rush" but before a mutual commitment. Those old but acutely painful memories of having been betrayed haunt us, so it may be difficult to complete a task or keep a commitment to oneself. Or, it may be hard to move on, knowing that it is time to move on but being frightened to let go of what is known and predictable.

I WAS SEXUALLY VICTIMIZED twice before I was six years old. The first episode was actually one that lasted a few months.

He was really nice to me, showering me with attention and physical warmth, knowing that I was hungry for stability and touch. However, he twisted that need to serve his own needs, and although he did not hurt me physically, he did hurt me by disappearing from my life, with no explanation. I guess

I was still so young I didn't grasp everything or anything for that matter, so I must have still been looking.

The second episode was rape, and I was temporarily silenced. I mean I retreated inside myself and I hardly spoke to anyone. I was unreachable really, but still normal enough to get by, so nobody really suspected anything except that I was in need of a positive male role model in my life.

But what these two episodes taught me was to steer clear of trying to let any other man get close to me. The second man hurt me so much, I just figured it would just keep getting worse.

We were abandoned and we also abandoned. Some of us abandoned parts of ourselves, hiding and denying the pain, pushing away the feelings, losing opportunities for help because we could not trust. The young victim may unwittingly alienate himself from others so that he feels even more alone and isolated. This sense of isolation can remain with us through adulthood, making it harder to seek help and creating difficulties with long-term relationships.

I THINK I TESTED a lot of men in my life to see how far or how bad I could be before they would give up on me. I didn't have to wait too long. And during my life as a child, adolescent, and adult, I failed a lot of men, like uncles, employers, supervisors, so that I lost out on plenty.

I HAVE DEALT with my issues regarding abandonment in the following ways. Because I was so filled with fears and anxieties over being tossed aside (because that's exactly what happened to me after he was done with me but not before I was feeling emotionally dependent on him), I learned to put up with a lot of crap.

In seeking ways to survive and recover, some of us became rescuers, trying to make certain that everyone would be safe and secure. Sometimes, we choose to withdraw from a relationship quickly and with no warning. Sometimes we jump from one idea to another, one job or person or thought to another.

Some of us assumed an abandonment mentality. We may have tried to create a world of isolation and solitude for ourselves to avoid further abandonment. If I had learned, even wrongly, that I was not good enough to hold onto a significant adult, then I might assume that I truly am worthless. Through this thinking I abandon myself. The broken boy grows up unable to understand his own self-estrangement, his feelings of loss and rejection.

I STOLE. I grew up trying to buy people's attention, especially my mother's because she was hardly ever available for me. That's how another adult was able to so easily enter the picture and take me over. Well, I'd steal and then give her my goods. I also had to lie about how I got the money for the stuff, and she never acted like she doubted me. I stole to keep her in my life, as poor as it was, because I figured that's what made the difference. So, even now I will shower some people with presents when I'm in one of my manic spending moods.

I became a fire starter. So much of the time he kept me, us, in the dark. It was all so dark and I could not see. He avoided light, never letting anyone see us together, and he acted so ashamed when it was just the two of us. For me, fire was excitement, and lots of people would come to see. Nobody ever came to see before. But you know what? Fire starters stay in the background, in the dark, or else they get caught. So there I was, still by myself.

I have this overwhelming feeling now as I am better able to recall the specifics of my ordeal that something was being taken away from me. Each time he visited me in my bed, I think I must have felt that he was stealing from me. It was the way he'd leave after he was done with me. Always quick to withdraw and go. I can still feel the chill in the room after he left. (To this day I hate it when someone leaves, turns over, or walks away.)

Anyway, when he was gone and I was all alone again, I would fantasize about how someone else would come and stay if only . . . I could never figure out if only what, just that I must have to do something more. It hit me that if I had games or food or toys for him, he would stay. But I didn't. So, I guess I must have figured that I would need them. But he was long-gone before I started to figure that one out.

I figured I could steal money to buy things and I could bring food to bed. No one came, so I ate the food so no one would find out. I got more food and I ate it all. I got really fat, so as a teenager, I was very overweight. Nobody liked me. Hey, it worked, right? I mean, at least I wasn't hurt again. Everyone just left me. Alone.

I DEVELOPED PRETEND CHARACTERS who became part of me. That's called multiple personalities. I kept mine till I was about thirteen. I think by that age I was feeling safer, but I got ahead of myself. These characters had names too: Elizabeth and Victoria. They were sisters. And I was them and they were me. It is very hard getting back in touch with all this. I never told anyone before. But I guess I'm feeling okay. They were English girls and most of the time I was Elizabeth.

I think they came to me a little while after I was raped by a friend of the family. He had so admired me. I can still remember how proud I felt that he was paying so much attention to me and that he was pleased with how soft and fine and pretty I was. He was a real pro at this. I never felt put down about being compared to a girl. He never called me a girl, just admired how pretty and soft I was. There was a lot of stroking and fondling of my body parts. He was really always so cool about the whole thing, saying how he wished we could always be together forever because we belonged together. He was my pal, my idol.

He was dating women, including my aunt, so I didn't see a problem. They could get married and live across the way from us. Yet I think I did get his drift, that this wasn't going to last forever. If I was a girl, it would be perfect. But that's really crazy, only I didn't know that then.

Well, this one time, he brought me out to a wooded area to go swimming and he said we could change in the car, which is what we did. When he was naked, he made sure I could see his erection. Then he starts mumbling about no good women and some other stuff I don't recall probably because I didn't understand any of it. Then he starts his touching and feeling of me which I was used to, only now I too was naked like him. And he was making it all seem so natural that day too, just him and I in his car with him getting more and more excited and insistent and becoming more focused on what he was wanting. But he was gentle as always so I didn't really think about what he was making me do, that he was forcing me or hurting me. He just seemed the same guy.

After he finished we went swimming and we kidded and played as usual. Back in the car, later, he made me do it again, which I wasn't so crazy about this time. On the way back he seemed different, and I can see even now his sad eyes. And I was thinking it was because of me. Now I think the whole filthy mess was only an act. I was supposed to be feeling sorry for him because of what we did and I was supposed to feel sorry that I couldn't be a girl, his girl.

He moved on soon after this, and it was some time after he stopped seeing my aunt and me that Elizabeth and Victoria entered the picture. Outwardly I was a boy, but inside I was Elizabeth whose sister Victoria was our best friend. We talked to each other and ourselves and my fantasy world was rich with their stories. And still I maintained my boy-self. I was sometimes picked on by older boys because of how they said I acted, kind of like a sissy, but I tried to ignore them and then maybe not act like Elizabeth when I was out. I was very quiet in school, but there were no problems. They were separate for the most part.

As I reached puberty, and my body began to grow and change, I just remember that one day after my thirteenth birthday I said good-bye to them. And they went. I think too that carrying that load was getting harder and harder for me to do, so the time was right, I guess. I let them go. They didn't abandon me. But they were girls, so I didn't expect them to. And as I became more male, I suppose it was safer for me to say good-bye. I haven't thought about any of this for years. It blows my mind that for about six years I had a secret identity, like another personality, that nobody could touch. They left and I was left with a very lonely, shy, mixed-up and scared kid. And that sucker got away!

Victims grow up, but we don't outgrow the hurt and old ways until we see what we are doing and search for alternatives. In one respect, change is threatening to a man who had been a victim of sexual abuse as a child because it implies abandoning a set of responses that may have been effective. There is safety in predictability, even if what may be predicted is harmful.

We also need to learn that if we abandon old ways we are not abandoning ourselves. Nor, should we be too hard on ourselves if we begin to grow out of a relationship which might have been holding us down. Growing out of a relationship is not abandoning someone. What we work toward abandoning is that sense of utter helplessness, dependence, and addiction in interpersonal relationships.

No More Heroes

For many boy-victims of sexual abuses, the notion of hero has become a disappointment. A hero is someone we admire, look up to, and wish to emulate. There is a useful book written by Gerzon, entitled, *A Choice of Heroes*. I remember trying, as an adult, to understand what had gone wrong in recent times so that there are few heroes. I was not even considering my own lack of a hero, not then.

THE HEROES I'VE CHOSEN for myself, and I didn't always realize consciously that I am a survivor, were usually gentle men. For example, Alan Alda is a good candidate. I feel I can trust him. But growing up in the fifties, there were no Alan Alda's, so I was stuck with the likes of John Wayne. Women were more likely to be my heroes, which was great, except it was hard to admit it, and almost without exception, they were brought down by some guy.

In order to have a hero, two basic elements are required. First, there must be a positive role model and second, there ought to be self-love. I believe if we identify with the first, the second develops. For many victims of childhood sexual abuses, both were lost, often together.

I USED TO FANTASIZE that someone was going to come and rescue me, keep me safe and warm, and then I would be happy. He never came of course. So I try to be someone else's hero, but it doesn't work because I think I'm not yet my own hero.

Often, in the aftermath of betrayal by sexual victimization, a young boy is confused and frightened because he has lost a hero. As we have explored in other sections of the book, there is a playing-out that occurs; we search for our fantasy hero. In our recovery, we learn to love ourselves more and to become our own hero.

Double-edge sword of broken promises:
"I'll be back."

As victims we followed or even pursued acts and attitudes which reflected through a distorted mirror the manner in which we were treated. Consider the poem, *Rescue Mission*:

sitting on a curb, shyly watching a man tinker with his car engine, i dreamed

he smiled big and spoke with an ease and comfort about this and that

i held each tool before i'd hand it to him memorizing its name and shape

sometimes i kept it in my small hands too long and he'd have to ask me twice.

the year was fifty-one or fifty-two, and the summer city heat laid down on us

a hot breeze moved little as passing cars left us breathing in their fumes

we didn't mind as the air between us warmed with our words and laughs

i wanted so to keep him there so i could know more about him and his world.

his work done he sat on the curb next to me arranging his tools

i could smell him and see his sweat-drenched oil-stained hands and arms

he wiped his forehead with his hand then reached over to reclaim his wrench

i wanted so to keep it forever between my heels and the curb so he would stay.

we talked a while longer, he and i, about cars and tools and ice cream cones

a summer day long ago when all i wanted was to keep him like a tattoo in my life

instead he left with a promise he'd be back with a tool set for my very own

and i sat on the curb each day all summer waiting for my superman to come back.

they all thought i was crazy that the sun had gotten to me good that summer day

no man had stopped to fix his car and talk with me and
promise to return
no man was going to teach me words for tools and engine
parts and life
no one believed that he'd come back to me yet i knew he
would someday someday.

i got a little toy motorcycle with its very own rider dressed
in policemen blue
and i named him johnny so quickly and so assuredly they
laughed at me
one pocket held the motorcycle and my hand held the
seated plastic figure
who in my heart was warm and loving and very real and
very dear to me.
johnny came back and we would go together to saturday
matinees
always careful to keep him hidden so i wouldn't lose him
like the wrench
aware also that i had to take the motorcycle with us so no
one would ask
how come that little boy is so attached to a little blue
plastic cop?
i stopped standing at the sidewalk waiting and waving for
him to come back
one weekend i had stayed overnight with relatives and my
plastic cop was gone
no one could console me or understand that my little heart
was broken then
when they found part of him on the floor and another
part in the puppy's mouth.
they all thought i was crazy that the sun had really gotten
to me that day

too many matinees and popcorn candied apples and too
little sleep
perhaps i'd fallen on my head leaping from the bed to the
dresser top
no one believed that he'd come back only to be killed in
the war.

Promises are paradoxical for us. We make them because we
feel we must, even when we know we cannot possibly fulfill them.

I'M TERRIBLE. I'll tell someone I'll meet them somewhere and I never do. I get too scared. Lots of times I don't
even call them. Guess I'm afraid it'll happen to me. Again.
That's how it was with me. I got promises of "next time" so
much, I stopped believing.

Or, we seek promises from others, which we believe and which
they sometimes use to keep a hold on us.

I DON'T KNOW WHY I'm like this, but I believe
practically everyone. I have this blind faith, someone once told
me, and you know what happens? I get crapped on. I lend
people money and clothes and they tell me they promise
they'll get it back to me. And they almost never do, and I keep
looking to believe them. I fall for the promise.

A victim may mistake a helper for another perpetrator. Since
most perpetrators are males, it is not uncommon for a boy to
react negatively to a male therapist. Helpers need to be aware of
the enormous sense of responsibility, guilt and shame victims feel
as they rehear the adults of their younger days admonishing them
to be more careful, to know better or know more.

I MEAN, I WASN'T just going to open up to the first nice
person, you know. That's what got me in trouble the first time.

He was a neighbor. It was dark and cold and he offered me a ride home in his car. It was nice and warm inside and I didn't mind that he pulled off the road and parked, keeping the engine running. He was all over me so fast, I wasn't sure what was going on or what was going to happen. It was over fast too. We didn't talk much afterwards, but the bastard had the nerve to say I should be careful hitchhiking. I never told because I thought I would get punished for doing what I was told not to do, hitching a ride, even if it wasn't a stranger.

These memories create very cautious, self-protective, and tight-lipped males. Paradoxically, in some instances it creates risk-taking males who laugh in the face of dangers. We did not know then. And some may be in the dark still.

Disempowerment has thrown us off center.

A friend, after I had told him I was working on the manuscript for this book, asked me to talk about the spouses and partners of victims. Another friend expressed concern over her not understanding the extent of her partner's pain and other reactions he (a former victim) would experience. Time and again, in my own life, I feel an unsteadiness within myself that interrupts my calm. The numbness we had to adopt and the depressions that masked the misunderstood angers revisits. They take their toll on us physically and emotionally, socially and spiritually. The process of recovery does not guarantee the elimination of these old responses. However, to acknowledge and have them understood helps minimize their power.

Early sexual victimization changed us. Our perceptions of our perpetrators changed; our self-concepts changed too. No longer would we trust them, others, or ourselves. We may have felt at the time, and for long afterward, that the change was permanent. We were transformed into "bad," "trash," "damaged goods," "faggots," "little sluts," "momma's little man," and a host of other epithets that were forced on us. We may have also felt that we were special or important to other family members. We might have been "seduced" into thinking we were saving a younger brother or sister from the same fate.

I DON'T THINK I ever believed anyone would or could love me, or even if they should. Our courting was very long and very slow because I could never believe that any of this was for real, that I would wake up from this dream, and she would be gone, leaving behind a note for me that told me exactly what she thought I was about. Still, there are times when I still feel this way. Trouble is, I have a hard time admitting this.

In previous relationships, which could last as long as seven or eight years, I would go on these binges where I would sneak off for a weekend with someone I hardly know and we would hole up in a motel room and have nonstop sex the whole time. But that was very different from how I would be with my current lover or spouse . . . very.

If I told her everything, I believe she would kick me out even though we've been together for over sixteen years.

The stage was set long ago for unwanted, unplanned, and unclear changes. The original assaults would revisit without warning too. Change therefore might be both threatening and welcome to the victim. Our reactions may be better measured and understood in degrees rather than in frequency. Some labels such as "manic-depressive" seem to help in illustrating this point.

IT'S MY MOOD SWINGS that really get in the way. I get very depressed and anxious. There are days at a time when I can't move, when I can't seem to get off to work. All the time I'm getting ready, she's saying hurry up, what's the problem, did you stay up again watching TV? I move through a fog then, walking as if I'm pulling my feet up through quicksand, and I'm scared. Usually we end up fighting because I say she doesn't understand, which is correct, but I don't tell her.

What would I say? Well, for starters, I would say that it's like somebody sneaks up on me and grabs me and spins me through the air as they hurl insults and threatening comments at me. When I land it's as if I'm coming out of a drunken stupor, dizzy and nauseous and not knowing what's next. I feel weepy, needing to cry but wanting to hide. I shout a lot because I can't hear myself clearly and there's this horrible deep humming sound in my head. And I don't have the ability to say, but ohgod how I wish I could say it, please be patient with me. I wish you could hug me, but not right now because I feel bruised and so supersensitive. I need air and space, and ohgod I need you so much. I never say any of that though. I think because I'm afraid of being rejected, for seeming weak, for admitting I can't do it on my own (which of course I can't).

My lovemaking is sporadic. I can go on marathons and then there could a moratorium on sex for weeks and weeks. I don't think it has much to do with sex drive. Sometimes I think if too many demands are being placed on me sexually, I run away. I should be flattered, but I get scared. I know that is confusing and even hurtful, but I can't help it.

We instigate change for the sake of change. The problem is that labels like "manic-depressive" often close off doors to discussion, masking the underlying reasons for the sudden shifts in mood or changes in behavior.

I NEVER WANTED to be predictable. And yet it was order that I cherished and hoped for. I thought that if nobody could predict me, then I was safe. If you knew what I wanted, what I liked, what I was like, then you could use that information and hurt me. So I ran away from that, yet professionally I became the "mortar that held the brick foundation together" (as one colleague described me once); I was indispensable. But, in other more personal areas, I would struggle against being labelled. Those qualities of course drove me from one rocky relationship to another. I changed for the sake of changing.

Puberty was very hard for me. The changes were so public. Everyone knew. I figured if it was beginning to show, so was the other stuff. When we were expecting our first child, I began to freak out. The first couple of years together were great. We loved each other and we had a real good time together. When I found out she was pregnant, I got scared. I mean I was very happy, but I was scared. People thought I was scared of the responsibility, but it wasn't that. It was being public. Isn't that weird? We were married and everyone knew we had sex, right? But this was different.

I went through a period where I was sleeping around. And I did it with both men and women. I guess I wasn't sure, right? The perpetrator was a man, a relative, and when I started changing and growing, he changed toward me, and ended up not coming to me anymore. I was scared of girls, but I was curious too. My cousin hit on me a couple of times, like he knew what had gone on between me and my uncle, who was his uncle too. Anyway, it was like I was going through my earlier years again.

I changed toward my wife because of the changes, and it was a very hard time for us. I never wanted to touch her then, and it was really awful. After her third pregnancy, she figured out what was going on. Another change is we got a divorce.

The term 'excesses' is also used in this section to help us understand some of our long-term responses and reactions. Some of us sought comfort in drugs, alcohol, clothing, food. Some of us sought to be excessively thin (using jogging or running, choosing an ascetic lifestyle) or to be accomplished at something. Some have identified this tendency as overcompensating or as overreacting.

A change occurred, sometimes as a radical transformation of our lives, more often as a gradual disempowerment guided by an offender. This knocked us off-center for a long time to come. The process of surviving involves building self-awareness and self-acknowledgement, plus regaining control of the direction of our change. As we look into ourselves, we begin to appreciate the inner strength and power from which we may draw and grow.

[[4]]

CHAPTER

Forgetting But Remembering

Engaging the Victim

There are the original offenses against the young boy. Whether they involved exhibitionism, fondling, or penetration, the perpetrator usually acted in a series of steps that lead to the offense. There was a kind of softening or preparing for the kill, finding a mark, looking for a likely victim. A perpetrator of sexual abuse is a careful observer, skillfully using conversation, feigned interest, or gifts to gain the trust of the unsuspecting child. Most offenders have had much practice: those arrested have reported as many as 70 or 80 victims.[2]

AS A YOUNG BOY, I was carefully and slowly seduced by a man in the neighborhood. He ended up becoming friends of my family, but his contacts were through me first. It's like I brought him home, if you follow.

Well, over a period of months, he worked his thing on me. He was good company. I learned to trust him. I could go in and out of his house, and since my parents were out a lot, he was a convenient thing for them too. They never questioned

---

[2] See for example the Segal and Marshall study (1986).

anything about him because he was well respected and he didn't "act funny."

He was great fun to be with, and I looked forward to him so much. I even stopped seeing some friends because I wanted to be with him. I would run over his house after school sometimes and he would even get me to do my homework. So he was even considered a good influence over me! Over time though he's kind of testing me, I think, although I didn't think anything at the time. Little secrets between us. A secret handshake. A magic coin. Treats before dinner as long as I would eat my whole dinner at home.

The events preceding the first intimate contact between perpetrator and victim are usually light-hearted. The boy is lured into a situation in which he progressively loses control over himself. This stage has been termed "engaging the victim." We often think of this stage as involving someone outside the child's family, seeking to establish a bond.

AFTER ALL, HE WAS THE ADULT, and he was so sure of everything. The way he drove, the way he moved, he was really masculine. He brought me farther and farther away from the safety of my parents (with their permission) and I became more dependent on him, for transportation and food on these day trips, so when it happened, I had no choice, no escape hatch.

The male perpetrator may be threatened or challenged by some aspect of the boy; he wants to "straighten him out." Or, he may be attracted to a young boy's vulnerability or sensitivity, yet react to it violently or destructively. If the perpetrator is a female, she too may be motivated by the power issues of the male perpetrator, using her sex to control the young boy.

WHEN I WAS GROWING UP, I was sickly. Lots of problems with my stomach and bowels for example, so I was used to my mother taking me to doctors and being in the examining room with me. My father was never with us on those visits, and when I'd get sick in the middle of the night, even when I was 13 or 14, it was her who would come to my room and help clean me up. Sometimes she would even give me a rubdown while she laid in my bed next to me, rubbing my back and shoulders, and I can remember times when my stomach was so sore she had me lay on my back and she would rub my belly. Sometimes I'd get a hard-on, and she would tell me not to worry, it was perfectly natural, and she would hold me and rock me in her arms. She never touched my cock though.

One time I was really hurting, and the pain was in my groin. I was about 15 or 16 at the time. She told me to let her see, and I was really shy, so I said no, but she sat down on the bed next to me, and told me she was my mother, that she loved me, that she had seen me naked before (no matter that it was years and years ago!), and she gradually lowered the blankets to my thighs.

I was really embarrassed but she was so convincing, saying she just wanted to make sure I was all right, that she wanted to see if I was swollen or if the color was different. So I agreed, but when I started to undo my pants she said no because I must be so tired and weak (after all I was in bed still dressed), let her take care of me, and she undid my pants, and slid them down. I can still feel her hands resting on my hips and it was her eyes that really got to me. She was pulling down my shorts and she was kneeling on the bed because she said she had to get them all the way down so she could see everything, and her eyes never left that area.

She said don't worry about having an erection, we would just wait for it to go down, and then she started asking me to show her where it hurt, and telling me to tell her what part and she would touch me all over there saying, "here?" And I couldn't help it. All of a sudden I came and she just said that was okay, it was natural, and she would leave me alone now. But she said she bet I was feeling much better. And I was. And she would ask me how I was feeling a lot since then, and I would always say fine, and she would say, "Are you sure?" She said that my father was too busy to tell me about the changes real men go through, but that she as a woman knew too, and she could help me.

And one other time, when she had waited up for me to come home from a date and I was in a really pissy mood because this girl was a real pain, we sat on the sofa and she (my mother) laid on my lap as I told her everything. When we both noticed that I had a hard-on, she patted me and said that was okay because we knew about it and why didn't I go get ready for bed (she knew I slept in my shorts) and she'd fix us something nice to drink.

I was standing in my room in just my shorts when she came in with some Pepsi or something and told me it was okay; it was like I was wearing swim trunks. We sat on my bed and she kept eyeing my crotch, watching me get harder and harder. We were talking, and then she curled up next to me and then leaned against my chest. She admired the way I had grown, and although she never again came in contact with my cock, I felt like she was making love to my body. Then she got up and said good-night.

I was so horny, I shoved my hands inside my shorts and started jerking off. The door swung open, she smiled and said she forgot to take the glasses from our drinks back to the kitchen. Then she smiled again and said good-night. I started trying to avoid her a little although we were always very close.

I started college and her office was nearby, so I would stop over to visit her, and I discovered that one of my buddies was spending a lot of time in her office. I found out later she was screwing him. And I thought that's what she wanted to do with me. I've had numerous affairs with married women, all ending after a few rolls in the hay.

The hurt is deep and painful. Many victims lose trust, and in its place come fear and disloyalty.

I AVOIDED TEAM SPORTS because I would never trust anyone. I just figured my team mates wouldn't protect me. And I was so afraid of being caught, I would want to bolt and not follow the planned play.

Lack of trust may manifest itself in later relationships as a lack of commitment or unfaithfulness. It may occur both as a response by the former victim or reappear in the responses of those around him. He may seek relationships that require loyalty but repeat the offense by disappointing partners. He may seek and find relationships in which he apparently demands complete loyalty or monogamy, but choose partners for whom these expectations are unreasonable or unrealistic.

SO OFTEN I WOULD FEEL I was losing some part of me when I would start to get close to someone. It wasn't limited to a sexual thing either. I just used to feel that if I gave, I wouldn't get back, that people don't reciprocate.

I was the pleaser. It was my job to always make sure that everybody else was happy. I know that this is true of my early abuses. My mother always had to be pleased, so that I was not allowed to do or say anything that would upset her. So, I never told her what was happening to me. And the man who was abusing me wanted only for himself to be satisfied. And if I didn't do it right, he'd get upset, like I was really hurting and failing him. And it never seemed to be good enough, but I was so confused I kept trying.

In my work, I still take it very hard when somebody voices displeasure or disappointment. It's easier for me to do just what has to be done, and get out, and that's the way I've been in relationships.

The offenses may have ceased, yet they continued in different forms. The victim represses the abuse, usually because of disbelief, fear, confusion or pain, so that numbness and amnesia replace recall. The boy still hurts and he hides, trying to avoid those who might hurt again as well as those who might know.

SOME PARTS OF ME really did remember while other parts forgot. The latter saved me while the former shaped me in so many inexplicable ways.

Not remembering is different from forgetting. The young boy has little choice other than to forget. The perpetrator orders him to forget and so do adults who just don't want to acknowledge that something is wrong. As more former victims disclose what happened to them, the cycle of self-protectiveness and defensiveness is broken.

WHEN I FIRST BEGAN to realize what had happened to me, I remember telling people that I thought that was what had happened, that it all seemed like a dream. Imagine trying to convince adults, when as a child, those are the kinds of impressions and perceptions one has! Those might be the only kinds of feelings one has. As the realities grew, and as an adult I felt more inner strength and support from others, I was better able to discuss details. Still, I was like a reporter, giving the details, with little emotion. I was both remembering and forgetting. How could that have happened to me? Why did it happen? Where was everyone else? And perhaps most important: Was he right in saying and doing those things to me because I took it instead of fighting back and winning? So, second-best, I kept quiet, showing little if any feeling. Yet there were the signs.

People need to know what those signs are so that love, support, understanding, and trust may be applied like salves to the soul.

Inconsistencies in the victim's stories, when they do describe what happened, are usually due to the cycle of remembering and forgetting rather than lying. It is unfair to allow the clever adult mind of the perpetrator/defender to argue against the victim/plaintiff. The perpetrator is trying to make his victims forget while he tries to remember his lies. The victim is trying not to remember the realities of the attack while he tries not to forget that he is a victim of a crime that he does not understand except through the filters of adults.

Internalizing

There is a beautiful and appropriate statement that affirms that children act and become what they have seen and felt. This is so true for victims of sexual abuse. In response to these experiences, neither fully remembered nor totally forgotten, many victims perform a circuitous dance through life.

As survivors, we identify how sexual victimizations altered our perceptions, expectations, and interactions with ourselves, with other men, and with women. The loss of power and control was so traumatic that later in our lives even a hint of threat evoked avoidance responses. So we acted based on incomplete or distorted information.

It is different from having fallen out of a tree and recalling the danger, learning to be more careful. It is different too from being caught by your parents while "doing something wrong." Here there is closure: punishment, correction, reactions. The family's reaction to a boy's sexual abuse is often a strong conspiracy of silence. For victims of sexual abuse, the event lingers.

More Offenses: Replaying Old Acts

When, without warning, a heavy sadness falls, followed by unidentified danger and depression, a sort of search begins again, with the same kinds of hesitancies and dreads and fears. One little word or act can set off such upsets and tears it is difficult to fathom the depth of the hurt.

I REMEMBER being with a partner and at the moment when emotional intimacy and physical intimacy were escalating and merging, I freaked out. Something in the way I was being touched, something in the way I was feeling, created such a panic, such an awakening, I couldn't go on.

We may relive aspects of the offense. There is a tendency to recreate part of the event as the victim, the perpetrator, or both. This replay may be a valid depiction or it may be an opportunity to alter something. Thus, the victim may act as he had, as he wishes he had, as the perpetrator had, or as he wished the perpetrator had. Each of these is combined with his partner's reactions, which too may reflect an aspect of one or several of those identities.

There is also a tendency to recreate part of the event by assuming a role or position of someone we may have wished was present, a rescuer. We may also play out roles as an adult in which we not only are rescuers, but we are excellent listeners, astute observers, or advocates. Sometimes, we play out the "perfect" parent roles with our partners and children.

We must acknowledge and accept that the early victimizations taught us well how *not* to take care of ourselves, especially in interpersonal relationships. We are unprepared. We need better "teachers" than some of us were given.

Victims of sexual crimes may learn seductiveness. Unfortunately that learned behavior sometimes confirms perpetrators' and other adults' perceptions that the victim should be blamed. The young boy may use or try to use "seductive" mannerisms to hold onto a person or to avoid hurt. The older male, working to survive, may use physical attractiveness seductively. Unaware of the roots, he may inappropriately use it, confusing attractiveness with power.

Another important issue is sex without love for self and others. If someone's sex had been used against us (and we may have taken half-a-lifetime to discover this) with little or no love, then we may react by either doubting such a connection exists at all or by insisting that there must *always* be that connection. In either case, if we do not love ourselves first, then we risk repeating the offenses against ourselves.

Another common reaction of victims, once they reach adult-hood, is to become preoccupied with compensating for some deficiency or deprivation they think enabled the original offense.

I ASSOCIATED MY DEGRADATION with poverty. It happened in a foster home and again at a camp poor boys went to for a week in the summer. I just figured that was how it was. I fought to move ahead, and I always knew I would. I got to be the best, and I don't let anyone get on top of me. I mean, that's the way I see it. No one will top me. I'll kill if I have to. Not really, but I am very competitive.

Over and over the victim meets offenses and offenders, through interactions with others and when he looks in the mirror. He sees parts of a troublesome puzzle he does not yet quite understand. The secrets have been buried for so long, and even when fresh in his younger mind, they were distorted by the offender. Children do not have the vocabulary, nor do they possess the cognitive skills required to understanding the psychodynamics of sexual abuse. In a young child's eyes, the cause and the effect of the act are shoved aside and deep deep away.

I WAS NUMB for a long time after it happened. I wasn't even sure what if anything had happened, but I did feel that whatever it was or wasn't, it wasn't good. I felt ill. I had a stomach ache and I was dizzy. I went to sleep and when I woke up I was different. I mean, I felt and acted different.

For a while after, they said I must have had a high fever during the night and when it broke I must have suffered a little (and I'd see eyes roll and their fingers circling their temples, as if I was crazy). Since I didn't know for sure, I started to be crazy, acting out, getting in fights, but as soon as I was reprimanded, I'd stop and just get quieter.

So, I went deeper and deeper into myself, just like that time I went to sleep. And for a long time that's the way I'd deal with things. I'd just get up and walk away if I could, and doze off. Most of the time, people just figured I had too much to drink, which was usually true. Like that song says, some of us drink to remember and then some drink to forget. I'm really very isolated though.

Recollections and Revelations.

Victims repress. That is one way to begin to survive the loss, the pain and the hurt. The memories go under, in a sense, and they do not surface for a long time. It is a form of denial. I think many sex offenders know that, perhaps because some of them had been victimized themselves. We are told as children to forget this-or-that. It'll go away or get better. It is easy to see how a child-victim chooses this route.

NO ONE WOULD WANT TO HEAR it anyway. Most of the time, parents just seem too busy.

But the man who has survived often has flashbacks. It is by dealing with these revelations about the past and about the present, regardless of how painful, that we become better prepared to make a better life. This awakening to consciousness is a first step. Often, a trained counselor may serve as guide for our clearer understanding of what the experiences have meant to us in our lives.

IT WAS VERY SLOW for me. I didn't just get up one morning and say, "I was sexually assaulted when I was a kid. That man who I trusted hurt me forever." The awakening took a long time.

I awakened from one nightmare to another, so lots of times it was just easier to go back to sleep. I think I may still do that even though most of it is now out in the open. Some things are still too hard to talk about or think about, so I close my eyes and it's all over and it's okay

I realized I had been assaulted a couple of years ago. And even though some things were beginning to make a helluva lot more sense to me as I realized that was the truth, I still preferred at times to go back to sleep, to be numbed again. Because the truth is this is very tough, very hard. It's like first going through a kind of confession even though we're not guilty and then being ashamed and angry that we did it or let it be done, and then trying to accept that we are okay even though we feel pulverized, and still we need to look at the past and the present. I have learned that so much of what I have done in my life has, in some way, been related to having been sexually victimized as a youngster.

The awakening occurs in stages, similar to the stages of grieving. There is only just so much we can tolerate at any one time.

SOON AFTER I AWAKENED to the realization I had been a victim of sexual abuse, I dressed differently. Really plain and drab clothes. It was as if I as the adult version of me as a boy was redressing myself so I would be camouflaged and therefore protected. This lasted several months and it was after some counseling sessions that I realized what was happening to me.

I keep a journal. I've kept journals for years, recording experiences and feelings, using my journal as a way of talking with myself, sharing private thoughts and emotions. Usually, my entries are pretty detailed, yet here are excerpts from portions of my journal, soon after I realized I had been sexually victimized. The first entry wasn't recorded till almost a week after I awakened from the nightmare:

"Everyman's private literature: memory " (A. Huxley). oh, so much. not sure I want to write. more memories filled with pain, smack me against the head. why me? then. and now. why me? I will see [the name of a counselor] 4/8. More pain. more shame. and anger. I need to know how to cope.

There was the shock. Also, I can note the degree I chose to intellectualize, as with the citation of an author. I read like a telegram, probably afraid to write at all.

It comes slowly, very slowly, as if recovering from a coma, a heavy assault that wounded me not just once (then) but now again. why does it happen? why does it (all? or is there more to come, I hope not!) come? And why does it hurt? when will it end? every word I write comes out slowly. and it hurts. oh, God, how it hurts. I see that little boy, so innocent, so quiet, so frightened, and what else? I don't know. Do I want to know? I know I'm afraid. But I am also very angry. Why——how dare anyone——would anyone hurt, molest (that word took me a <u>long</u> time to write) that kid——<u>me</u>! How do I deal with it so I can move ahead, away from it. I hope M. [name of counselor] can help me. I really do. I'm too tired right now. I'll return later. No more secrets.

In the previous entry, I am so vulnerable, so in need of help and guidance.

Talking with M. was extremely helpful. He suggested that I write about the incidents, even before I talk about them. Let my heart do the writing. [SO HIS EYES CAN DO THE LISTEN-ING?]

I think I was being protective of both of us. In one sense, the advice I received from my counselor was good. I can recall that session, filled with my pain and with my shame. I also recognized his discomfort as I told him——or as I began to tell him——what had happened to me. I became angry with his limitations only long after that meeting. I was disappointed; I wanted him to make it all better.

I am very sensitive; I feel vulnerable. It's too hard to write now. Later. I am literally crazed. My thumb aches. Shit.

I was trying to do something for myself, but it was very hard. I was feeling very lonely too. I was feeling as if I was the only one.

I continue to awaken. Still I lapse into restless sleep, dreams, and deeper sleep. Bits and pieces of a life half-lived emerge and I am overwhelmed by sadness. I grieve still. I have some unfinished business I need to resolve. I need to resolve it so I can move on, and I feel that I cannot accomplish that. Part of the problem is that more stuff comes . . . Pain. Confusion. Who was I? What was I? . . . I was abused.

I am reexamining myself. I am looking at that kid who struggled to survive. And I am even more sensitive as a parent to my child's life. I want her prepared and protected. I try hard not to let my craziness affect her. I am aware of that.

Still, the crazies and the ghosts do come out to haunt and hurt me. I try to control them. It makes me very sensitive and vulnerable. And this could help me with her. I need to be less afraid. This sensitivity and vulnerability also affects me with S.

I am still not ready to share everything with her. Part of it is her. She needs to have some space. It is a heavy issue, but I will work to resolve some and trust more and share more. This is threatening because it strikes the heart and soul. I know it hurts. And I also think part of her wants it to be over.

So do I, but first it all has to come out, to be released. I want to be empty of the dirt, the foul feelings, the hurt, the pain. I want to fill up with sunshine and flowers and soft meadows. I want to swing in a hammock, gliding through space. I want to be resuscitated. Perhaps even reborn.

In the previous entry, I am afraid. I know I feared for my child, that such an ugly and horrible thing could possibly happen to her. And I feared for myself, wondering about who and what I was. I was afraid I might have been gay.

Questions of sexuality are very important to pursue and answer, preferably with a trusted and caring counselor. We are exceptionally vulnerable during this awakening stage, and it is important that we feel safe and accepted.

My last statement is crucial: I wanted to start all over, to be born as someone else. Evidently, to have been brought back did not seem to be enough.

I'm tense. and I'm tired. How much longer and how much more deeply do I need to go before I discover what I need to find and move on? How much more do I have to know before I can let it all go? I know I'm afraid that this area opens questions about my sexuality. That's very frightening. And threatening. I'm afraid, but I want to know. I want to be whole . . . Still the most frightening thing about all this is that I feel as if I was different from how I appeared because of the secrets held inside me.

So, once again, there is the issue of sexuality. Later I wrote:

*I even felt healed enough to make love; it had been so long
a time. I still have my pain. It fades, but I've had some nightmares, bordering on night terrors: one night, a narrow, spiral-like
staircase became narrower as I ascended. I awoke gasping for
air. So, the fear, the panic, remains.*

As we awaken, the depths of depression may create an
emotional anaesthesia. To make love might connote healing and
wellness, yet the freedom and sharing might represent a threat.
Awakening is painful, yet it is necessary for one's recovery. Our
minds served us well by holding back those thoughts and feelings
until now. We must be ready, if our mind——that which had
protected us so well all that time——is slowly opening, slowly
opening us.

PART TWO

THE MENDING MEN

[[5]]

CHAPTER

Talking and Listening

Boys don't talk.

Males should hold it in, keep it to themselves, don't let go of
the control. Boys don't cry either. Male role models also encourage boys not to allow anyone to get the best of them, and if
it happens, not to let them know it matters.

A major thesis of this book is that how males respond to
sexual victimization is directly related to how they view men and
masculinity. The more rigid the sex role representation, the more
difficult it will be for the victim to come forward. There are many
socially implicit rules that prevent males from becoming close to
their male friends. Becoming too close to another male may raise
questions about the "sexual standing" of an individual and will
exacerbate homophobic responses. This phenomenon sometimes
prevents the male victim from disclosing to another male what
happened.

Sexual abuse and rape are not unrestrained physical expressions of love; they are aggressive sex crimes. The young boy does
not know how to make those distinctions, so he may fall back on
what he feels and hears and understands at the age of the trauma.
Consider now the predicament in which the boy-victim finds
himself when he is the object of sexual victimization.

I WAS THIRTEEN years old, in eighth grade. There was a bunch of us in the car with this teacher who was taking us to a safety patrol meeting across town. And he asked me to sit up front with him, and all the guys, even my friend Buddy who was sitting in the front seat with me next to the window, started snickering. And when this guy puts his hand on my thigh, and I start getting a boner (that's what we used to call then!), I'm feeling guilty, like it's my fault that this guy is liking me and what's worse I must be liking it too. And he's driving along, using one arm on the wheel, looking straight ahead, not even acknowledging what's going on.

I begin to move away, and it is then that I know he knows what's going on, because he slides his hand higher and increases his grip on me. So I sit there, staring ahead, letting this teacher hold me. And all the time I'm thinking that my friends know and they're figuring it's my fault, that I must be doing something too. After all he's the man.

Later, he may continue to need to block as much as he can of the experiences because he finds no support from those around him.

As we begin to experience, consciously or subconsciously, some of the effects of this victimization, we may hurt ourselves because we blame ourselves. And for a very long time, we may not forgive ourselves. We forget who is the real perpetrator.

FOR A LONG TIME, I hated myself. I hated my looks and I hated my body. I thought that I was too short, too small, too fat, too weak, too pale, too smooth-faced. For a long time, I wanted to be someone else, anyone else! And then, as I began to awaken from this ugly nightmare, I realized that I really did want to be someone else because I figured no one else had been made to go through what I had when I was younger. I was looking for escape, and I found it in different ways.

This book addresses the issues linking a boy's sexual victimization with the male role. This connection often explains why reports of sexual abuse occur infrequently and help arrives late, if ever.

THE FIRST PERSON to really listen to me was a wonderful and sensitive counselor. It was really hard to tell her everything, and she stayed with me throughout it all. And when I was all finished (for the moment, at least!), she looked at me and said, "I am so sorry that that happened to you, so sorry you had to go through all of that pain," and we wept, mostly me, and I told her that she was the very first person to have ever said that to me.

Permission to Tell

The process of telling our stories is difficult because we had been told (ordered, threatened, frightened, or emotionally coerced) not to tell, and the old echoes may be quite loud at times, although nobody but us hears them. It is very important for us to tell, the sooner the better. Remember, though, it is *never too late* to tell. In one respect, that is what this book is all about: telling what happened so that we may begin again.

For me, part of the healing process involves my giving myself permission to tell. Most victims lack that sense of security. Often, I act as a catalyst for someone by showing how he may empower himself. When he is ready, he will begin to tell.

As I have said, males in our society have not been encouraged to self-disclose emotions and worries. It is helpful to remember that and to give us time. Believe me, it is easier (but never easy) to talk to someone who is patient and accepting. As a survivor, I know that the telling is a painful and embarrassing event. Other men I have listened to have reported similar feelings of shame and confusion, fearing a breach of trust or a misunderstanding.

I WAS VISITING with some cousins, and, as usual, the topic of parents came up, and of course we began to talk about my mother, who had really been a pretty strange lady, especially when I was younger, much younger. And one of the recollections someone had was how nuts she would become if I was late from being outside. My cousin's wife then asked me why. Was my mother being strict or controlling? I said I thought it was both, that she was very strict with me and that she wanted to control my entire life.

Two things became clear that evening as my cousin and his wife and my wife and I visited: Much more talking and telling has to go on (but we couldn't that evening because my daughter was at the table and it just didn't seem the wisest to tell her to leave the table.) But we all will talk because I want to tell my story.

The second thing that became more clear to me is that I am pretty certain that my mother knew at some level that twice in my life before the age of six I had been sexually molested by men. It may be that she just did not know what to do or how to deal with any of it, so I think she was trying to prevent it from happening again. But because she did not confront it openly I didn't, and I went through a series of hells for most of my life. Until I began to tell. Have I told her? No. Will I tell her? I'm not sure.

We hold it in, and we are clothed in guilt and shame; horror and disbelief. How could that have happened? How could I have let it happen? And that is what many perpetrators predict: we will not tell. They have the power and they can take away our innocence and our ability to speak. They have that power until we know and we believe that we can tell.

WHEN I FIRST STARTED to talk about it, and that is exactly what it was like, a great big IT, I was very uncomfortable and ashamed and bewildered, so I know I was filled with lots of pain and confusion and that could have made my listener uncomfortable, even incredulous. But at the time it was so important that I talk and they listen, and I was so much in need of warmth and support.

Often, for whatever reasons, I was received with blank stares or with silence and topic change. I got so upset that people whom I considered close were being so distant, I wrote a poem, '*duly noted*', in which I described myself as feeling like a recording, a newspaper reporter, listing for the listener, who, minutes ago, had tuned me out, the feelings I was having, and they were becoming disjointed and incomprehensible more and more as I knew I was being heard less and less. That pain of further silences and denial was perhaps hardest of all to accept.

I was in counseling for a while when this opportunity came up. It took me quite by surprise. During the semester, I was giving this student a lift from one campus (where I was teaching a course and he was working part-time) to another campus of the university (where I worked full-time and he was taking courses). Anyway, he was an interesting fellow, full of nice chats and conversation, and I enjoyed the company.

This one week, while I was driving us down to main campus, he started talking about baby-sitting some kids this past weekend. He said that all of a sudden he was getting concerned because they did a lot of rough-housing and wrestling, and although no one had ever said anything to him (he was around 21 and they were 10 and 12), he thought maybe someone would think he was touching them in the wrong ways and that they would say he was a child molester. I mentioned earlier that I was in counseling at the time, and this is important because I was going through a lot of conflict, pain, and shame about "telling" anyone "about me," as if I was the one in the wrong. My counselor and I had been through this area on a few occasions, and she was very supportive and gentle with me, applauding my attempts as well as my disclosures with others.

Well, here I was in the car with this guy, and I was feeling okay about everything: about me, about the issues, and about him. I asked him what he thought and felt first. We talked about that for a while. And then I heard myself say that I think he, the boys, their parents, and I all knew the differences between bad touching and good touching, that I for sure knew because I had been sexually abused as a youngster. And he said, "really? Wow, that's terrible," and we continued talking, leaving one topic and moving to another.

As he was leaving my car, I told him that I rarely had talked about my own victimization, but I appreciated the opportunity to talk with him because I think it would help each of us. I felt so relieved and so proud, proud of myself, probably the proudest I was feeling about myself as a human being in quite a while. It was okay to tell. And it still is.

Are there repercussions? Yes, sometimes. The telling of our stories is cathartic. Disclosing what happened provides us with one of the first authentic opportunities to begin to express our sadness, shame, and anger. Telling may be difficult, yet we know how it can help cleanse us of a grime that weighed us down. The process of telling may often begin with ourselves, hearing and listening to the messages: "Yes it had happened to me," and "Yes, it had to be buried for a long time," and "Yes, I am going to feel and be better," and "No, I will no longer hurt."

What we do as a result of our self-realization and acknowledgement varies. The common experience is to reach out to another person. It could be a counselor, a friend, a partner, or an associate. We continue to reach out as we reach inside to clean out this dark and hidden closet, gathering strength and courage, affirming ourselves as victor and not victim!

To Learn Again the Meanings of Words

I have always been fascinated and awed by the power of words. A young child utters sounds representing a word and an idea or action is recorded. Words confirm love and comfort. Words are what we learn so that we may learn. Words teach, whether spoken, written, or signed.

Words also may wound. As children we did not understand everything that was said (or not said) to us. Sometimes words created more questions and self-doubts, more fears and shame.

He said, "*do me.*" Never said what it was we were doing. "Do me." No one ever said what it was he did to me. Sure, he hurt me.

I still can't say the word "*suck,*" like with a straw or something. It became a very dirty and disgusting word for me.

I asked him what was he doing, and he said, "*nothing.*" Sure wasn't nothing to me. But I felt like it was supposed to be nothing and I was therefore no one, not there. And then neither was he. It was like he was denying the whole truth of the matter. He was violating me. He was invading me, pushing and pressing and fondling me.

She said, "I am your mother" in a stern voice, and I was supposed to obey her and do what she demanded. "*Mother*" is a dirty word to me. It was dirty; she was dirty; I was dirty.

Queerbait. I was that. But he wasn't queer. But I was queerbait. He was gonna fix me. It was like I was supposed to be broken and that's why I was called queerbait and this was how he was doing it?

Girl. That was the word everybody could use so I would confirm. Very strong word power. I remember seeing the movie, *Exodus*. I was a teenager at the time. And there's this scene with Sal Mineo, and he's telling what happened to him in the camp. And he's crying and he says they used him like a girl. And the next part of the movie I forget. I just focused on what he was saying, over and over in my head: "used me like a girl." And I held on to that, and it was making sense to me that he was crying because he was "like a girl." And I thought that's me too. It was really disjointed, but at least I was getting a message to my brain finally that very bad people did that to boys like Sal and me. Nazis.

"Good-bye" is one of those words that used to send me into great panic. I was being left and abandoned all over again, and it was horrible. I would do practically anything to prevent someone from doing that to me. And it all seems so irrational now, but "good-bye" was a very threatening word to me.

Rape. That's something that happens to women. So I didn't ever use that word to describe it. But then one time someone said to me that's what had happened to me.

"Let's play." That's how it would always begin. His game, his rules. So now I hear that and I still feel myself shiver. It's like Jack Nicholson in that movie (*The Shining*) when he says, "Here's Johnny." It still can get to me. Let's play.

Words also may offer strength, understanding, and control. They also help explain and clarify. Some words that we consider in this section have connotations and denotations, suggested and literal meanings. Once a word is spoken aloud, it may help build a platform for understanding, coping, and recovering.

"Molest" is one of those words I block. Whenever I hear it, I think of mess. I don't know why, but I just see it that way, being messed up. I know I was sexually molested because that's what they told me much later, but it sounds so clinical. When I started to tell, when I was coming out of my prison of silence, I halted and stumbled a lot. I said he had touched me; he held me, fondled me, kissed me, felt me, and I kept hearing the word, molest. And I thought to myself, no, he didn't mess

me up like a rag or anything. I needed those other words to make it real.

When I was an adult, I remember reading "*Midnight Cowboy.*" And there's this part where the hero, the one played by Jon Voight, is tricked, and he is sexually molested in some way. I say that because the author uses this really indirect and euphemistic language. But I knew what was happening as I read and reread that part, so he did get his point across. Yet I want it to be more direct. I want him to tell us what the other character's mother means when she tells him that's the only way he's gonna get it, by knocking Jon Voight unconscious. It then becomes a dream sequence. An ugly one, for me.

The most healing words said to me were: "*I believe you.*" And, "*I'm sorry that any of that happened to you.*" I had carried my secrets inside for so long, keeping them buried, and I think I had been trying to hold in the lies, protecting everybody. I also think that when I felt ready to tell, after all those years, nobody would believe me or the pain I was feeling. To be assured by a friend that I was believed, that I wasn't making up any of that awful stuff, helped me unburden myself.

I had the victim mentality for so long that when the word "*survivor*" started to get used, I had a little trouble with it. I pictured those sad pictures of people who had been forced to be in the Nazi death camps, and I said to myself, "Yep, that's how I feel. I beat death, but look at me now." I refer to myself as one who is surviving, who continues to survive. For me, the term "survivor" is a label that does not seem to give credit to the process of recovering and healing. Not enough.

Words can hurt. Words can heal. The words in this book are presented as affirmations and also as guidance.

Accidental Kindnesses:
"I think she knew something was the matter."

Outsiders, those who don't know, may show a little kindness to a boy and he may not respond in a way they expect. This section deals with signs of abuse and constructive ways to help a boy talk freely. Most survivors will recall such accidental kindnesses and may offer suggestions.

I REMEMBER FEELING singled out and that feeling was very frightening and threatening. I know she meant well, but it was too much to handle at the time, and I fell in silence. That's the way I recall this.

I was about nine or ten at the time and this first grade teacher at my school struck up a conversation with me on the bus. It turned out we were going the same way so we even got off at the same stop and waited for the next bus and got off at the same street again, where she invited me to join her for an ice cream soda, which I did. I was feeling so confused and scared. Here she was a teacher, so I had this feeling that she was safe and I should obey her. I was also tempted by the treat. But I knew I shouldn't talk to strangers (but she wasn't really a stranger) and I shouldn't take gifts (but it was only an ice cream soda). Also, she was asking a lot of questions, I thought, and I was holding inside lots and lots of secrets.

I think she knew something was the matter, that I was a troubled child, very lonely, very quiet, and very nice too. She just didn't know how to reach me. I don't think she could have, especially in the way she did.

I wish she had referred me to someone, yet I wonder if that would have worked. Maybe if there had been a program at school that taught children how to prevent assault, that would have a period afterward when children could disclose, maybe. I just needed to know that I wasn't alone, and I was feeling alone, and with that teacher I was feeling terribly alone and isolated and pointed out.

I once cut out a great cartoon, from *Garfield*, who talks about what a great friend his "pookie" bear is because he's such a good listener. Garfield says that's because he has two ears and only one mouth, implying we ought to listen twice as much as we talk. I agree. People in the lives of victims (and surviving people too) need to listen. Hold off on the advice for awhile. Listen.

Kindnesses are also expressed in offering a "safe place" for runaway victims of sexual abuse. We must remember that their perpetrators often provided their shelter. Kindnesses are also expressed in how judges conduct their court rooms and attorneys treat the boy-victim. We all should remember too that survivors need and want kindness, yet they may feel unable to ask for it.

When Someone Tells You

I am interested in human communication and in how people are blocked, how they hold back. I am also interested in how listeners may become blocked and hold back, as if the words of the speaker could or should not reach them. There are sections of this book that are painful to read, sections some will skip over because of discomfort. I know too that there are sections that will be read over and over again, perhaps because they are so painful, as affirmations for survivors.

When someone tells you that he was a victim of sexual abuse, listen and believe him. It is neither your job nor responsibility to remove the pain or to try to make it all better. Yet to listen and to let the person talk and tell you whatever he chooses about the experiences is a precious gift, something personal and fragile. Self-disclosure creates the ultimate sense of vulnerability and poignancy.

We who survive know how broken and shattered we have felt for so long. We may have tried to build up walls, but there was always a chink that remained. I believe this is for a reason. We needed a time, an opportunity, and a person.

SEVERAL YEARS AGO, I was feeling so scared, but I was so blocked inside. I was desperately afraid of personal loss and abandonment. I was petrified of being rejected. I was terrified of being alone.

I ended up alone, and I could feel myself go through a number of changes. My heart started beating really fast. I was having trouble catching my breath and I was shaking all over, as if I had this great chill. I began pacing back and forth, back and forth, and I had trouble seeing and hearing, as if I was in some kind of deep tunnel, at one end, at it was getting darker and more remote. I thought I was going to die.

I managed to contact a friend and she believed me when I said I needed her help right then. When she saw me, she told me I was having an anxiety attack, that I would be okay. I did a lot of crying and some talking, mostly about some recent events that had involved my being hurt by people I thought I knew well and trusted. I remember images that frightened me, like huge ugly monsters that would come and hurt me and take me away forever.

And my friend stayed with me, wrapping me in blankets and holding me and soothing me with her presence and her words. And I can still remember that when this awful pain in my chest (the right side, I remember that, so we didn't worry about the heart) was beginning to go, as if being lifted, and a smile appeared on my face and I wept now with relief mostly, I said I wanted to keep a little bit of that pain to remind me, so I would remember to pursue this. It's like a little stone inside my chest, always the same spot, and it visits me. I use that as a gauge on my emotional well-being.

When somebody tells you, have few expectations. Just be with him and listen. You may be told anything, something, almost everything, or almost nothing. Be patient. And be touched that you have been selected, for there needs to be a high level of trust present for any level of self-disclosure to occur. Listen to the silence as well.

Notes to Partners

When you care about someone, and you feel that person cares about you, it is difficult to understand, accept, and address the many issues that arise from a history of sexual victimization. It is further complicated because often the memories were denied or distorted in order for him to have survived.

I offer few suggestions for partners because if you are reading this, you have already taken an enormous step in the direction of being there for the man who is working to survive and recover. What we do need is love; unconditional love. Love us for who we are at a particular moment; not for who we might or should be. We also need support as we struggle to understand what has happened to us.

There will be changes, most, if not all, for the better. He will express anger over what happened. He also will feel damaged, untruthful, ashamed, and afraid. Be patient. Be available. And remember to give him time and space.

WHEN I WAS AWAKENING from my nightmare to the recognition that I had been sexually abused as a boy, I can remember her pain and her discomfort. And I can also still see how she wanted to protect me, so as I struggled to find the word, she tried to soothe me and encourage me to try to forget it. But I had a need to tell, and she did listen. I think when I began, with all my hesitations and signs of discomfort and pain, she thought I was confessing an infidelity. And in a way, I felt that I was. But she never left my side, till I asked her to, and although lots and lots of times she said she didn't really understand what I was saying, she stayed with me and accepted my tears and angry voice, seeing and knowing I was getting professional help.

The key words are listen, patience, acceptance, and love. I don't think, unless he asks for it, that he wants advice on how to feel or act. I believe that what he still wants is someone to love him, a need and feeling whose source lies deep within the little boy lost and hurt.

[[6]]

CHAPTER

Reevaluating

Darkness: A Prison Keeping Us Inside Ourselves

Rape victims are raped more than once, and in more than one way. There is the violent physical act of dominance and disregard, and then there are the outcomes, short-term and long-term. The short-term outcomes include how we were treated by the perpetrator afterward and how our self-esteem and our self-perceptions were altered. The long-term outcomes include how we coped without the conscious awareness or the support related to the sexual victimization.

The long-term effects of sexual victimizations vary, yet the common theme is dysfunctionalism in some aspects of life. This may involve poor interpersonal relationships: problems with intimacy, commitment, sex, and trust. This dysfunctionalism is so common that it produces a near-universal need for a survivor to reevaluate his past and its hold on the present.

As we move toward recovery, we may need to revisit old times and remember past moments, bringing them to light in the present. Parts of us existed in silence. As we grow and move away from the prison keeping us inside ourselves and into the light where we are freer to look at ourselves and others, we begin to discover what we had not known as youngsters. As I awakened from the nightmares of childhood sexual abuses, I acquired knowledge about myself and about others, past and present, so I would be more secure.

Part of the process of recovery is to become the adult we needed then to help the child within us now. We need to move beyond the role of victim. This process involves a reevaluation of old thoughts and fears and a clarification of who we are or who we may become. It is very important that this stage in recovery be acknowledged and understood. When I maintain a certain self-image for me and for others, I perpetuate a belief and attitude that may have little validity or basis in the present. I need to trust change just as I need to trust a decision to remain.

As victims, we were told many things about ourselves, much of which had no truth. If I was called a "girl" or a "faggot," I may have responded to either of those labels in a way that was appropriate for my age and understanding. As I grew up, silently fearing, even at a subconscious level, that there was some truth to the label, I may have struggled in response to the label. A male struggling with this fear, only partially understanding its source and genesis, fights or yields; in neither case does he understand himself.

It is not "wrong" to be gay or straight or bisexual. But it is unfair to the individual to have remained in a victim mode, struggling with unresolved fears and feelings, doubting himself and his sexuality. A careful and honest appraisal will help.

I DIDN'T KNOW I wasn't a homosexual until I was in my early twenties and I started dating women, and then I knew for sure, but it was killing me inside even then that I was an object of some man's desire. It was only later, after a number of broken relationships (a few with other men because I still wasn't sure), when I was in counseling that I found out a number of myths victims have about themselves.

For me it was unlearning a lot of negative stuff. I didn't know that I was able to sustain a relationship, whether it was sexual or not. I didn't know if I was straight (I am). And I didn't know if my father was (he is). I didn't know what a great effect his abuses of me had on just about everything I did or tried to do. And I didn't know if my mother knew (she still claims she didn't).

A sense of powerlessness is part of the foundation for the prison many of us found ourselves in. The perpetrator took something of us away and he held us captive to our own fears, confusions, and sometimes, if we were young enough, a near-total incomprehension.

I HAVE IMAGES and sensations, nothing really clear. I was still sleeping in a crib. I see that because one of the images is shadows from the crib bars. But you know what? I think it could have been the playpen. I don't know, but the next thing I feel is being gagged, choking, not able to breath, and . . . I just don't know any more. I still block. A lot of people don't believe me because I never finish the story.

As victims too we did not know how to stop the abuses. "Just say no" is inadequate to propose as a remedy. We are not discussing peers of equal status, weight, and power. We are not discussing being offered the choice of taking or not taking a substance. There was neither free nor informed choice for the child-victim.

IT WAS LIKE HE WAS digging through a pile of rags and my naked body was at the bottom. I'm not even sure I made the connection between what I saw happening and that that was me. I didn't even realize what he was making me do. And then I say, hey I was nine years old.

This is a complex problem, and there are no easy answers and no simple solutions. Greater knowledge of how childhood sexual abuse occurs, especially for parents, is a critical first-step. The accounts of former victims repeatedly confirm this.

IT TOOK ME YEARS before I realized that I had been lied to, manipulated, and taken advantage of. Over the years this went on, right under my parents' roof, it was like I was having a nervous breakdown.

It began when I was around twelve. He was sixteen. It started out innocently. He was so sophisticated. He knew everything. And it was really easy because we lived in the same house. First there was exposure. He made me feel envious and inadequate. But I was also curious, so when I stared at him, he began to twist the situation around. He made me touch him and then he got me to jerk him off.

Once he hid in my room and after I was down to just my shorts, he jumped out and we began to wrestle. He was naked. I got an erection and he pulled it out through my fly, and his touching was exciting me so much. He changed positions so my mouth was next to his penis and it was the first time he forced me to give him a blow job. He made me believe for the longest time that I was a faggot because I got so excited that day. And then he would always grab my crotch and when I would get hard he would say, "see you want it," and he would force me to take him all the way in my mouth.

Over the next five years he did this to me almost every night of the week (he dated on weekends). He would come into my room, and sometimes it would be early in the morning or it could be at night, and sometimes he even did it both times, and he would check my crotch and if I faked sleeping or if I was on my belly he would turn me over.

This went on so much I really believed that he was right. I always had an erection. Nobody told me different so I thought that I was queer for him and that's the way life was. I avoided most people, had no friends, and I was a mess.

One time when I was in my senior year this girl asks me to the prom. I didn't know what else to say, and since I was getting a reputation as a faggot at school anyway, I said yes.

My parents were really happy. My father even lent me his car and gave me a lot of money. But he never talked to me about sex. I guess he figured my brother must have told me. Yep, he sure did.

My brother was pretty quiet those two or three weeks before the prom but he still came to my bed almost every night. He just wasn't as insulting. The prom was real nice and my date was too. She was a good dancer and she said she would teach me. It was a slow dance and I got really excited and I got a hard-on. And then I got real scared. It was like, oh no, he's here even now. I started shaking and then started acting crazy with her, saying I wanted to go. She said okay and we rode around for a while.

I said I wanted to take her home but she said why didn't we park somewhere. I had heard stories in the locker room about girls and parking, but I really was naive. Anyway, she starts at my zipper and lifting my cummerbund, and I don't know what to do. I mean, I'm excited, I'm curious, and I really want to go on, but I'm also scared. It's like I'm with my brother and I'm waiting for him to make the next moves. So I let her.

And so I'm sitting in the backseat of my dad's car with my pants and shorts around my ankles and then she takes my hand and puts it on her lap. We end up masturbating each other and it was like I had discovered gold! She was really funny about it too because she said she had never seen a guy act like me. I got embarrassed about it but she was really sweet.

When I got home, and returned my father's car keys to him, I went upstairs to my room. I didn't bother to turn on the light, I just got undressed. My brother had been waiting for me in my bed. He was naked and so was I then. He didn't touch me. He asked me about the prom and my date. I told him. It was real strange. He listened. Then he moved toward me. I was riveted to the floor. I wanted to run or yell but I couldn't.

He reached for my cock and it was hard. I mean, I just told him about my date, but he turned it around once again, and said I was still hot for him. He began to push on my shoulders to make me kneel and I started to fight back, but I couldn't move and I couldn't talk. Then he pushed me and I fell on the floor. He jumped on top of me and grabbed my head and shoved his cock in my mouth. I stopped trying to resist. I just went limp. I didn't know how to stop him. The best night of my life and he was ruining that too.

After he was done, he laughed. He said it wouldn't matter how many girls I dated, he was the only one for me. Because I was queer. And he picked up my tux off the chair and he threw it at me and said to jerk off in it and then he left my room. But he came back, and he kept coming back until I moved away to college.

It has taken years of therapy for me to even talk about any of this. I haven't talked to him since I left home. What I have learned is that a victim doesn't know he has choices. That's the problem. If nobody else knows what's going on, then we don't know what to do. I believed my brother for years. I thought he knew all about me.

The events described by the previous voice confirm the need for more surveillance by parents of what is happening within a household; here, the relationship between male siblings.

FOR SEVERAL YEARS, I didn't even know what was bothering me. I didn't know I had been sexually abused. I blocked it. But the bouts with depression and my cold and distant behavior with people continued even though everything seemed to be going great. Then there was this big crisis in my life and it was like I found out I had been a victim. But I didn't know. Does that make sense?

It makes a lot of sense to the perpetrator that a young victim be kept in the dark about his human rights. But parents have a responsibility to teach children, from a very early age, what good touches and what bad touches are. There are a few books that are helpful, such as *Alice Doesn't Babysit Anymore* and the *Book of Touching*.

Locked in/Locked out

Locked in/Locked out; always alone. Victims do not know they can escape. They often cannot without the help of a trustworthy and understanding adult. Survivors of sexual abuse also need the assurances that they will not be trapped again. We need to know that we can maintain our equilibrium.

ABOUT TEN YEARS AGO, I was invited to present a paper I wrote to a national meeting. I was very nervous but I knew what I was doing, well prepared and all that. I was scheduled to present on the second day of the conference. So, the entire first day of the conference, over and over again, I studied the other presenters, the time they took, how they handled questions, and most importantly, I studied the exits. So, I would leave the meeting room several times to check out the doors, the corridor, and the stairs even! This was my first major presentation and I was so scared and anxious that up until the last minute I figured I would bow out, feign illness or something. I was a basket case. I was so afraid of being trapped and not knowing what to do or say. It was as if I was reliving the past without really understanding it.

I did get through it, and I was complimented for my presentation. Little did anyone know I was dying inside. And after it was over, all I wanted to do was escape, get back to my room, even pack and leave. I was so afraid of being stuck there.

Some of us are imprisoned within ourselves by our own fears and hesitations, limited or lowered views of ourselves and of our potentials. "No, I could never do that job" or "No, that person would never be interested in me." We are locked in. Locked in by ourselves . . . all alone.

I FIND THAT I have lots of anxieties, which have really kept me a virtual prisoner. It's been very hard being a man who panics and who is afraid to go out and be among strangers, in strange places. People expect you to take over, to be in charge. Dates want you to make suggestions about where we should go and what we should do, and most of the time I would be content to stay home, but that doesn't usually go over real big. I have taken sedatives to get through lots of this, and I also will drink to calm me down, but then that makes other problems for me because then I lose control, and that scares me too.

Inside me has been a little boy who has been imprisoned for years and years. I found him a couple of years ago, and I sometimes talk to him, trying to release him. It's very slow, and we are both very scared because what I already can remember about the sexual abuse is so awful, and I know my child's memory holds even harsher realities of those early days.

We have been bound by another's hold on us and sometimes there is that awful sense of having been trapped in a nightmare not of our own making. Sometimes, we have sought to escape this nightmare through addictions to food, other substances, rituals and people. It is when those means of escape are harmful, as with addictions and abuse, that we need to learn to deal more effectively with the pain. Recovery and healing help us to focus on moving the bars of the prison so we are released.

Some Fantasies Still Linger

Fantasies are an integral part of the victims's childhood. These fantasies often contain the themes of being rescued or being invisible. Sometimes these early fantasies continue to control our reactions and behaviors as adults. It is important to recovery to recognize these influences and reevaluate their significance.

THE WAY MY PERPETRATOR courted me, it was like a fantasy. I was ten or eleven, and he was this older kid (around nineteen or twenty), a college kid in the neighborhood who was working in a neighborhood center where I went to hang out. He was great, really nice and attentive. He'd show me all kinds of neat things, take me for rides in his car, and out for sodas. This went on for weeks and weeks, and since he was working in this place, nobody even my mother thought anything bad.

Summer was coming, then school was out, and he got permission to take me camping. This was like a dream come true because I had never been camping and he had bought me things for the weekend, things he showed me as we drove out of the city and into the country. He'd have me reach in his pocket for this, and that pocket for that, and soon he had gotten me to unbutton his shirt and unbuckle his pants to get a pen knife, which he knew I really wanted. I was so happy because I was having him all to myself, not having to share him with other kids at the center, and he knew this.

We got to this place way out in the sticks, and he parks the car, and just sits there, shirt still open and belt still unbuckled. We sit there for a while that way and I'm doing most of the talking because I am so excited and everything, but it's hot even in the shade, so then he says, how would I like to go swimming, and I am jumping up and down because I know he will be the best swimmer and he will teach me. He says to get undressed then, and we leave the car, and I follow him running through this clump of trees, and I lose him, and now I'm a little scared, so I slow down, and he jumps out from behind a tree and scares the pee out of me. He's laughing, but I think it's okay, and then he walks with me with his hand on my shoulder.

We get to the edge of this lake, and he takes my hand and we walk into the water together. I know he knows I can't swim, but I trust him so. The water is getting deeper and he tells me he'll carry me and to have him hold me is another dream come true. I've got my legs wrapped around his waist facing him and he's kind of bobbing us up and down in the water, and we're laughing and everything and then he kisses me. I'm surprised at first, but he tells me it's like we're brothers and I'm like a little puppy just lapping it all up.

We stay in the water like this for a while and then he says we ought to go back, but I want to stay, so he agrees. Then he says he's a little tired, so maybe I could float and he'll pull me around, so I lay back and he props my head against his chest and walks us backward through the water. Even now as I think of this I get excited because it was everything I had wanted. I had him and I was finally learning to swim.

We get to shore and the sun is so warm on us we don't even miss any towels. There's a patch of grass and he takes me to it, and he sits behind me and we look at the sun and everything. He asks me what I liked best in the water, and then he asks me how I had liked to be held. I think on that, and then say that I liked when we could see each other and he agrees, so he picks me up and straddles me over his lap. We stay like that and I can feel his hardness on my belly, but I don't say anything. I'm just happy to be with him.

After a few minutes, we get up and race back to the car, laughing and tagging each other. He says we can stay naked here, but let's pitch a tent, which he does mostly while I watch. He tells me to get the sleeping bags from the trunk, but I can only find one I tell him, and says well that's okay, isn't it, and I'm crazy with excitement because I'm gonna have him all to myself all night too.

He tells me to unroll it inside the tent and then he joins me inside. He says. "Let's see if we fit," so we get in together and he pulls up the zipper part of the way. He asks me if I want to face him so I crawl on top of him. He starts moving both of us around a bit till he says we're both comfortable, and I can feel his hardness again. I ask him about it and he says it's a gift, and then we're both quiet for a while. Then he starts moving some more and I feel him pressing my legs together real tight. He's kissing me and I just think how great this is, so I let him hold me and I listen when he says to keep my legs this way and he starts rubbing my back.

It's really warm and he keeps saying my name and I don't know if he's asleep or what, so I do what he said before and then he stops. Later, it's dark now, I feel sticky down there, and we run down to the moonlit water and wash off. We eat later and we do that thing some more over the weekend. He was paying 100 percent attention to me 100 percent of the time, and I never thought anything bad about what we did. He just told me not to say anything about him forgetting the other sleeping bag because it would make him look stupid. Can you believe that guy? Can you?

And now (referring to the statements above), I look back and I can see how very much I wanted to believe. I wanted to believe in him, and I wanted to believe in the dream, and I wanted to make it all so beautiful and romantic, and real. I protected myself, and because I did that, I've protected him all these years.

It wasn't like what I said. It wasn't. It was confusing, and dirty, and it was wrong because he had no right to take advantage and use me so. I was so frightened back then, afraid of the dark, of the water, and of losing him, and he knew all that. So, I made up the fantasy to protect me. And sometimes still I will fantasize about a lover or even about somebody who I get involved with in a work situation, for instance.

Some of us were so confused and hurt that we build a protective wall for ourselves, as the child and as the adult——the adult child——needing to trust and to believe. If we may have romanticized parts of our story, it was probably an attempt to shelter and protect ourselves.

MY FANTASIES INVOLVE CONTROL. I like to say no. But I can't. I get all swept up, and I just don't know to say no. I get overworked and underappreciated. In my fantasies, I am the king of no. And I am almost always a very powerful person with lots of men under me, so I boss them around and tell them no.

Some of us lived in a fantasy or through our fantasies to such an extent that we did not venture into the "real" world. It is very comfortable and predictable in a fantasy.

WHEN IT WAS HAPPENING to me, I would pretend I was somewhere else and it really wasn't me. Now I still have that fantasy, and more people get pissed with me because they say my body's working but my head's a million miles away. I guess I still want to escape.

However, fantasy is also very limiting, very inaccurate, and often inappropriate when one compares what is available out among the living. Among the living? Yes, because often victims live in a past without completely understanding it, and it is filled with ghosts and death.

I FANTASIZED MY FUNERAL more than once. I am young and the casket is open, and as each mourner comes to pay their last respects, they see more and more of me turn into a skeleton with huge snakes crawling in and out of my bones and openings. And they all know, and they wail and wail over my death.

When we recognize the fantasies and accept them for what they are, we may begin to appreciate our fuller potentials. It is also important that we realize that the kind of fantasizing that is repetitive or stereotyping further limits us. Fantasies are within our control, so we may be comforted by the idea that we are able to let them go.

Letters I Wish I Had Written But Still Can

There is so much unresolved for the victim, so little that had been possible to say or do. Now it is impossible to confront the perpetrator. But I want an apology. I want someone, anyone, to come to me and say, "I'm really sorry you suffered so much." No one has ever said that to me.

Some form of exorcism appears to help, often a letter we write to ourselves. There are other forms of emotional exorcism, too, ceremonies involving rebirth or role-plays, for example, which will be described in Chapter Seven. Here I will illustrate two types of letters: letters we wish we had received and letters we might write to offenders.

Here's a letter from that guy:

Well, here I am rotting in jail. They caught me, and I'm really paying for it. It's horrible and mean in here, but I deserve everything that's happening to me. I wish I didn't hurt you so. I'm sorry.

Here's a letter from Dad:

Dear Son,
I never meant to hurt you. I love you so much. I would never have wanted you to suffer. I know you can't forgive me

*or the lies and pain I caused you, but please find it in your heart
to pray for my soul. Maybe someday you will forgive me. I am
so sorry. Please try to believe me.*

Here's a letter to Dad:

Dear Father,
       *You did mean to hurt me. You were a no-good drunken
bum, and I don't believe for one second that you ever loved me
because you are incapable of love. I will never forgive you and
I will never pray for you because I hope you burn in hell.*

Here's a letter from my family:

Dear Mack,
       *We all are so sorry and we wish we could somehow make
it all up to you. We should have known. We should have seen.
We were so stupid and so blind. Can you ever find it in your
heart to forgive us?*

                              Love,
                              Your family

Here's my reply:

Dear Family,
       No.

I have been asked about my responses. Some say that accepting an apology or retraction is a sign of emotional wellness or
maturity. It has been argued that if the victim is to "get better,"
he needs to accept the apology.
       First, I respect a person's decision to respond to an apology
in whatever way or form he chooses. What I believe is healthful

and therefore potentially healing is that some aspect of the silence is broken. As a young victim, we were not given the choice to accept or reject the apology. It is the boy-victims for whom I am concerned. We were lied to. Our innocence, trust and security were stolen.

Second, why should I believe you now? You lied before and you probably lied to others too. So, I will not vindicate you; nor will I absolve you. Some of you reading these words may still not understand. I ask that you try. Many of the men whose lives and stories intersected with mine were working in positive and constructive ways to move on, to approach healing as a series of steps, helping the individual to move in several directions. When we spoke of letters or of conversations (real and imagined), it was with a lot of careful and conscientious consideration. Many of us were trying to reach resolution, to make peace. We were also struggling with remembering what we had been made to forget. The pain is renewed and it is raw. Healing is not covering it up (again). We are learning to respond as the adult we wish to become, remembering and protecting the young boy who had, in a distant past, been hurt and abandoned.

Third, knowing what I have known about perpetrators of sexual victimization, they are often repeat-offenders. Their acts are not limited to one time or to one individual. I ask myself if I have the right or the power to minimize their responsibility for the damage they caused when I cannot begin to know or imagine its full scope.

As a survivor, I may choose my own way of responding to those I hold responsible for my hurt and pain so that I feel safe and free to move on, to heal and to become whole. Each of us must make that choice, a choice we were denied in the past. People who want to help need to understand this.

One powerful experience I had was to write to me as a little boy. Some excerpts of those letters appear in Chapter Eight. That helped. I recommend that we write letters to ourselves, to the little boy and to us at every stage of our development until we merge in adulthood. When there are specific or painful or frightening issues, consult a trained counselor.

I look at myself even now and I know that I need to acknowledge the positive aspects of myself. I need to say to myself that I am a good person, that I like myself, that I have abilities and skills and qualities that are positive. I need to see and hear all that to believe it. Writing it down helps.

[[7]]

CHAPTER

Letting Go

We release the hurt so that once more we see and feel. First, there is the notion of letting go. And second there is that need—often not well understood—to retreat, to run away. These two ideas are actually related. If I choose not to let go, I am holding back or I am holding on too long or too hard. If I hold back, then I am not fully involved, so that I can run off and retreat more quickly and more easily.

Letting go involves living more in the present, less in the past or future.

I NEED TO APPRECIATE and to accept the here-and-now. Sometimes still, I am looking for the exit, scanning to assure myself that I am safe and that anytime I wish, I can get up and leave.

The survivor fears being noticed at these times, yet he is also afraid that no one will notice him either. "Notice me, so I receive attention. Don't see me, so you won't hurt me."

Recovery involves letting go of the anger, the pain, the memories, the numbness, the hate, the old grudges, and the fears. It also involved letting go of ourselves so there is less need for control. In interpersonal relationships, letting go is important since it signals a higher level of trust——of oneself and of one's partners. Survivors have learned to be very cautious, even though at times we appear reckless.

Letting go also involves expressing appropriate emotions, so that I will weep for what I know has been lost, and I will express anger for the right reasons at the right times. Letting go is a state of mind, suggesting a comfortable level of self-love and self-awareness.

Cutting our losses

There are losses during a victim's childhood as a result of the circumstances, situations, and people surrounding the traumatic events. Further, there are secondary losses resulting from the earlier losses. Most of us need to have time and often permission (mostly from ourselves, with the support of family and friends) to grieve and mourn those losses. It is critical that we respect this phenomenon, for it follows a necessary progression.

Since the molestations occurred in darkness and since we were made to forget and not tell what was inexplicable anyway, we must now seek a light to help us find what has been lost for so long, often for years and years

What is this loss? Actually, the better question is, "What are the losses?" He has lost power, control, self-esteem, innocence, love, among other elements of life. He has also lost memory. And what of faith and trust? And, what of the spontaneity and play of childhood? Lost. These are losses we may have searched to regain.

Death is so much more final, so much clearer. To have lost a loved one is painful, but there is closure. We mourn and grieve in the company of others, and often the loved one's name is spoken. We have feelings about our loss and the person, and we can talk about them. Whatever the circumstances, there is an opportunity to talk and listen, to interact and exchange, in a safe space. The loss a victim suffers is no less painful than death. Yet where are the mourners? Who hears our cries? Where are the tombstones for our own losses? Were we to find them they might read:

I THINK I LOST MY WILL. I just gave up. Most of it was inside me, so nobody really could tell. I just stopped doing things mostly.

I LOST MY VOICE. I mean, I stopped talking most of the time. I became afraid to say anything because his threats plus his strength terrified me, so I became very careful.

I LOST MY JOB. It turned out he couldn't handle it after he raped me. I was fourteen and it was my first summer job, and I really needed the money. But after that, he found excuses to find things I did wrong, and after a week or two, and after two or three more times with me in the storage shed, he let me go. I was so ashamed and so scared, and I think I was shocked too. So I never told anyone. And I didn't apply for a job for the next couple of summers either.

I LOST TRUST. Not at first because I was too confused and it was all so new. But after a while I knew he was wrong. I couldn't stop him because he was my coach and it was just "natural" for a coach to massage sore muscles! But not there, not where he was touching me. I was fifteen, I had a good future in football, but I figured if one coach was like that, they must all be like that. I quit.

And around a few years later I was doing something around the house when I sprained my groin, and they practically had to sedate me to examine me. I went nuts. The doctor who was examining me was really very nice. At first he thought I was being modest, so he sent out the nurse, but that just made me worse, so then he thought I was embarrassed by my size, so he moved away from the table and he just talked to me about different things. I was in great pain, but when he would move toward me or say what he wanted to do, I would start yelling. Then he said it was okay, I could just rest.

I started to doze off and he didn't touch me. He just stayed in the room with me. When I woke up, he was still with me, and I don't know why, but I started crying. He must have thought it was the pain, so he started to call for a nurse, but I said no. He turned around then. I remember. He just stood there and then I could see his face changing, like it was settling and changing color and form. And then he took off his glasses, and he wiped his eye. He said he wasn't going to touch me because he knew.

He said he'd give me a prescription for a pain-killer and he told me some other stuff to do and not to do. And then he said I should probably talk about it sometime because I was really hurting inside and that I was going to lose out on lots of things. Then he grinned, and he started to move toward me to touch me, I guess to pat me on the back, but I jumped up and put up my fists, and that sudden jump really hurt. He moved back then, asked if I was all right, and said to get dressed (I had removed my shirt), that his nurse would come back with the prescriptions and directions.

I saw him when I was leaving. He looked up and said since I was walking okay I probably was going to be okay. And then he said that that had happened to him more than once and he was a wreck for years till he got help, and he handed me a note on a piece of his note paper with the name of a therapist, and a brief note scrawled on the bottom: "All is not lost. Help is available. Good luck." Lucky I didn't look at it till I got in my car because I bawled like a baby then. And I took his advice too. Really helped. About a year or so later, I went back to see him to thank him, but he wasn't there anymore. Too bad.

I LOST TIME. I was so monopolized by my brother and so convinced I was gay, I hardly ever dated, so I was a real clod with girls. His abuse went on for about five or six years, until I told him I would kill him if he ever came near me again. He tried everything, but I just left home then, and he never knew where I was.

Then I started dating women finally when I was around twenty-two, and I regret how many lost years I had. It was tough too because I didn't know how else to act except the way my brother did. So I lost a lot of second dates too.

I LOST MY FATHER. My mother found out what was going on between us, and she kicked him out, got a divorce, and I haven't seen or heard from him ever since. That was over fifteen years ago. I miss him. That's sick, isn't it? No, not really. I don't miss his abuse, just my father.

The emotional connections with oneself and others are often severed by sexual abuse. The boy may retreat and withdraw, thereby denying himself the chance to find a safe and understanding place. He is angry at the perpetrator, but he does not act on that anger. Instead, he says to himself, "You're a bad boy and it's all your fault."

I NEVER WANTED TO SEE or talk to anyone ever again. I was so hurt and I figured it was my fault anyway. I was afraid it would continue or be repeated by someone else, so I hid. I lost friends then and it's still hard for me to make friends. I lost trust. He hurt me so much after I had trusted him so, I have a hard time now trusting myself. I screwed up once, so it could happen again.

Loss of power and independence result from sexual victimization. The traditionally male premiums on such qualities creates deep distress for many boys who had been sexually assaulted.

I SHOULD HAVE KNOWN BETTER. Everyone else stayed clear of him (I guess), but I was the stupid one who went on errands for him and delivered stuff to him, and I was the one he got. Looking back on everything, I see how he worked me.

He knew I came from a broken home, that I was a "latch key kid," and I was poor. He offered me money since he always tipped me for the errands and company because he started letting me stay after school to help straighten out the library. I was a loner so nobody on the street missed me and I was liking the attention and special privileges I was getting.

One afternoon, I was helping straighten out books on the shelves and he was handing me books from below. On that particular day he left the lights off but it was okay because the sunlight was coming through the drawn shades. Each time he handed me a book or took some from me he was lingering more, and I wasn't thinking anything much about it so I didn't say anything. Then he bumped into me and I began to lose my balance up on the chair and he grabbed on to me and kept holding me around my waist even after everything was still.

It got real quiet and I didn't know what to do or say. Everything began to happen so fast I wasn't sure what was going on at first, but then I knew what he was doing to me. I was scared and excited too. Here I am still in junior high and I'm getting blown. And it's a teacher. After it was over, he started crying, still with his head against me and his arms around me, and I don't know what to do. I want to get down and he lets me, and then he tells me how he's sorry, that I probably didn't like it, and now we can't be together anymore.

And it's like I'm the adult now, telling him how it's all going to be okay, no one's going to find out, we can still be together, and I can still be his helper . . . He's real quiet, listening now, and then he smiles and tells me or asks me really if it's all going to be all right, and there I am assuring him and giving him permission for more. That afternoon was just the beginning, but it almost always ended up with him being the child, sad and penitent, and me the father forgiving him.

Our boyhood losses have created huge and empty spaces inside us. Our actions as adults often have been attempts to fill those places with people and substances that only perpetuate the loss and the pain. We need to work to grow. We need to learn to nurture ourselves. Because at one time we experienced losses does not mean that we must continue to be losers. There is hope and there is help. What is most important is that we recognize the pain of our losses and the unlikelihood of regaining them, yet find the power to give ourselves additional chances and choices for a better life from now on.

As we anticipate recovering and healing, it is important to confront this idea of loss. Our earlier experiences may have taught us to "shut down," as a way of trying to hold on to whatever we felt was left. Perhaps we built walls around ourselves; or, maybe we tried to fit ourselves into a box, holding ourselves together, holding ourselves in. Those actions may have led to further alienation. We often became the "strong, silent type."

When we move toward recovering and healing, it is important to recognize that as we open and share we are not losing anything valuable. Rather, we are giving up some of the pain and anger. The connections with others surely help us with connecting with ourselves. What is lost is the mask, the wall, the rigidity, the hardness. As each of those disappears, we find the pieces that had been scattered and lost. We find that lost little boy.

Farewells

As we approach self-recovery and healing, we find ourselves making room. We clean house, finding and removing cobwebs, trash, and other old remnants of moments passed. As we recognize that there now is room for new experiences, new friends, and new ways of looking at things, we begin to say our farewells. While recovery is both painful and frightening it is healing and exciting too. We are beginning to let go, to let go of ourselves and the powerful pulls of the past that have controlled our existences for much too long.

I HAVE BEGUN TO LEARN to acknowledge and to actually greet my enemies——my fears and angry feelings for example. And I have also begun to let go, *to say good-bye* to them. Some fears have served me well. I had a great fear of intimacy, and it did keep me safe, invulnerable to pain and abandonment. And it especially helped me avoid closeness with other men. But I've begun to see that it has kept me far away from people, isolating me from people I otherwise would have known if I let myself.

I GATHERED SHELLS on the beach one afternoon. Then I climbed on some rocks, walking out toward the sea. At the edge of those rocks, I started to toss each shell against the rocks in the water below, and as I slammed each shell against the rocks *I began to say good-bye* to the pains and the angers and the fears and to all those I held responsible for my state. I ran out of shells many times over before I ran out of tears, many times again before I ran out of words. That afternoon was a good first step for me.

I KNEW I WAS STARTING to get better when I could touch myself. Crazy as it sounds, I had so much numbness and so much shame that I had to get rid of, I hardly ever felt comfortable touching myself, especially my penis. I began to tell all those old dirty thoughts I had had about sex and nakedness and my body in general to take a hike, and this one day I stood in front of a mirror and slowly undressed myself. I got really turned on, and instead of running from my sexuality, I stayed with myself, and *I would say good-bye* to shame, hello to beauty, hello to feeling good about myself, good-bye to suppression. Good-bye to fear of being discovered, good-bye to ridicule and humiliation.

I STARTED TO LOSE WEIGHT. I said good-bye to a poor self-image and to being addicted to foods.

For some of us, letting go of so much may be like an exorcism. For others it resembles blood-letting or releasing the poison from a sore. Whatever the imagery and whatever the form, the intent and effect is the same: to make room for a life that is more healthy psychologically and physically, socially and spiritually.

IT WAS DURING an all-night anxiety attack that I began to let go and say good-bye to the demons and ghosts who were occupying me. I said good-bye to cigarettes. To me they had represented an image of masculinity and toughness, a sense of immortality and invulnerability too. I was very addicted to them, and I saw that they were interfering with my self-growth and self-esteem, so I worked very hard to stop, and I have succeeded.

I've stopped calling and writing to certain people because they stopped reciprocating. I was doing all the initiating. I got tired of it, but I used to be so afraid of losing anyone, I would do anything. So instead of keeping the silence by not doing anything, I just wrote to them and said I guessed it was always one-sided and this side was moving on. I didn't say it in anger, just matter-of-fact.

It's been fine. Only one person responded and we have enriched our friendship ten-fold. It turned out that I was making room. Also, by being more direct and honest with this particular person, I said good-bye to some more old shames too. It turned out that he was thinking that I was afraid of his homosexuality, which I think I once was, but we were able to clear the air, and I guess I was even able to say good-bye to that too.

Find a bag or a box and fill it with imaginary objects and people. Then dump it. Fill it as many times as you need to, and when you think you have done enough, fill it and empty it one

more time. Then think about what you might like to fill it with
now that you have room.

I ONCE FILLED A RAFT with all the people who had
hurt me one way or another, and then I shoved them out to
sea with no food or oars or anything. It was a great fantasy!

Sometimes we need to say good-bye before we say hello. We
may need to learn to let go first. This is a sign of progress. This
is a positive step. We are learning to let go of the prisons and
walls and cages that have defined our identities and existence.

Letting go of anger

Anger comes; sometimes after realizing the full impact of the
abuse, sometimes in a period of depression and isolation. Since
males are not encouraged to vent their feelings through words,
their anger may be misdirected toward self or innocent others.

A friend whom I hadn't seen for a year dropped by unex-
pectedly from out-of-town for a visit. We chatted about many
different things, and had a wonderful time together. As he was
leaving, he told me how well I was looking and then asked me,
"What happened to all your rage?" I smiled and said that it was a
long story, but I was moving ahead with the issues surrounding my
abuse and I was healing. "I don't need it—the rage—so much
anymore."

We had been friends for over nine years. During that time he
had seen me lose my temper, break into fits of rage, overreact,
and fall into crushing depressions that rendered me powerless and
defeated. And although we talked about those times, we never
identified the sources of my anger.

When I started to realize that I had been sexually assaulted
as a child, and I told him about it, he was helpful by listening. He
was always a good listener. I saw too that he was a damn good
observer. I also saw that the path from victimization to survival
and healing to recovery was lighted by friends and counselors, by

reading and writing and drawing, and by a strong urge to get better, to move out of my sick bed into the sunshine. I did a lot of tripping and falling along the way, but I noticed that one barometer was the type and extent of anger I was expressing.

I don't hold back the words now. If I feel hurt, I tell you. If I don't want to go along with something, I let you know. It wasn't always that way. I used to keep my mouth shut and simmer and burn. Often I didn't even know why I was acting so nasty. And when I yelled and shouted, it usually caught people by surprise because they didn't know where it was coming from. Looking back, I think that it came from my having been unable to express my anger directly to the person who victimized me. There was always this feeling of incompleteness, that I would never be able to see him and tell him what I think of what he had done.

So I wrote an anger letter. I was shaking when the leaders of my therapy group for male survivors of sexual abuse assigned it. I never had to do that, and I was afraid of what I might say. I agonized over every word. But I did it. And I got such support and acceptance for what I wrote, for what I was feeling and must have been carrying around for so many years. I felt a release. I felt liberated, freed, untangled.

Part of the recovery process is defining our anger. We must work to understand and accept that this emotion was one of the few available to us at the time. Although we may still feel "out of control" when angry, we must remember that our concern about expressing anger may stem from control having been such an important issue in our personal histories. In recovery, we become honest about our anger and learn how and where to direct it.

[[8]]

Healing

It has been difficult for males in our society to ask for help with personal problems. We have not been encouraged to be introspective, self-analytical and questioning. Instead, we have adopted coping-styles that are outer-directed, action-oriented and success-bound. In doing so, we have not always learned to keep in touch with ourselves. The result of this for victims of childhood sexual abuse has been a sense of isolation and a denial of self. An important part of healing is to begin to say, "hello" to yourself again.

At a recent workshop I conducted for adult survivors of boyhood sexual abuse, I asked that we look at how we are today, how we used to be, and how we wish to be. This was helpful. Some of the men present had never before disclosed their stories to another man. This was unique. A brotherhood had been sought and formed. Trust was critical and it was assured.

As we talked with each other, and as we saw similarities in our childhood experiences and in our later feelings and reactions, it was important that we also focused on how we were that day. We needed to recognize the strength and courage it took to be there. We also needed to focus on the future, considering what we wanted. This part of the exercise too was very affirming. These are typical of the things that former victims want as they become engaged in the process of healing:

> *I want to take care of me. I might sound selfish, but I need to take of my physical being and my mental health.*

> *I need to learn to say no. Not that I won't do stuff for others, but I want to be able to have choice.*

> *I plan to take care of my body better, with exercise and diet.*

> *I plan to call a therapist.*

> *I've been in a very destructive relationship and I want to work on changing it, or ending it. I have a network of new friends now, and they give me the support to move on.*

> *I'm working up the courage to talk to my brother who lives in a different state. I think he also was abused, and I want us to talk. I want to tell him.*

> *I feel as though sometimes I've been a stranger. I've been a stranger to lots of people from my past and I think I've been a stranger to myself as well. It's as if I lost contact with us all, and that I have been behaving as a stranger to myself as well. It never hit me so hard as it has these past few months how separated I have been from everyone, even myself.*

> *I get in touch with the child in me. I don't mean to play. I want to do that too, but now I greet that little boy who was me and I let him know I love him. I had denied that part of myself for such a long time. I'm ready to deal.*

The importance of these statements is that they concern the future. Each statement represents an individual's commitment to taking responsibility for his own existence and well-being instead of turning them over to fate. If we recognize that many victims of sexual assault and abuse come from dysfunctional families, their fatalism is understandable. We have been more primed to accept our fates. This is the way it is (or was) anyway.

I believe this fatalistic acceptance, characterized by denial and minimizing the significance of the sex crime, is a functional delusion in which the offender and the victim participate together. "It wasn't that bad" is an anesthetic to emotional expressiveness and feeling. "Get over it" is a minimizing statement that victims have been instructed to follow. Threats and warnings hurled at the young male may have seemed "natural" in the dysfunctional family where he may have served as protector or helper.

One way we can deal with these issues is to confront our past, to become reacquainted with the realities of having been in an appalling situation under bad circumstances. The shrugs, the denial, and the isolation need to be redefined as a form of post-trauma syndrome. So, we need to greet all this, see it as it was, and reacquaint ourselves with ourselves.

I HAVE POWER. For me, I greet the offender and say in a loud and powerful voice, get out of here, go. I say that I will tell everyone. I get this new kind of power so I feel proud of myself. That kind of feeling I never had before. Or at least I don't remember, but I think I did because it comes so natural to me and I feel light and bouncy, like a kid. I guess I'm reconnecting.

Sometimes it takes a crisis before we pause and reconsider some of life's decisions and choices. It is not surprising since many males have been so thoroughly socialized to pursue, seize, and keep success that there seems to be little time to be self-reflective. On the other hand, some of us may have rejected the conventional male dream, partly because of low self-esteem or a disintegrated social system, so that success (as measured by some other's dream) is unattainable. What we all seem to have in common is that the dream is there. We are either drawn to it or away from it, driven to possess it or to reject it. The crisis may visit at the least expected time.

I RAN AWAY. I left home as soon as I could because it was awful. I left a lot back there. My growth was stunted, and I left some good people too. I used to blame them all. It was easier than saying who was really responsible, and that wasn't me even though that's what I used to believe.

Anyway, a few months ago, I called up home when I figured my father wouldn't be there. It was a Friday night payday and he was always out getting drunk. Anyway my mom answered the phone, and I started crying, but I got to say, 'Hi Mom.' And she and I cried and talked and cried some more, and she had to call me back and I wasn't even that scared he would find the number on the phone bill because I knew I'd blow this place and anyway it was a public phone. And anyway, it felt so good to hear her voice again. I also called one of my brothers who is married now.

Saying hello again is not the same as trying to go back to a former era, or trying to hold onto something long gone. Actually, this experience occurs after the farewells. To say hello again might let the little boy inside us see that it is safe out there, that we are able to take care of ourselves. That is a strong image, the one that shows the younger version of us needing protection and nurturance and, above all, love.

SEVERAL YEARS AGO, I was walking in a strange city. It wasn't a particularly bad place to be walking, in fact it was a connecting bridgeway between two hotels. But there was something so sinister in the air that evening that when I left the one hotel and crossed the street and started to climb the steps to the skyway, I could feel myself freeze, and I was shivering and shaking, having a helluva time even breathing.

I had heard several voices at the top of the steps and for some unknown reason, I associated them with danger to myself. I was petrified. I did manage to get back to my hotel. Nobody hurt me, but I was in poor psychological condition. I was in the midst of a panic, and luckily I still had the presence of mind to call a friend who got me through it.

One of the things we did was to take a walk along that same path I had taken the night before and I was amazed at how purifying and how reaffirming that experience was. I was saying hello again, this time with support and some degree of resolution as well as knowledge that I was ready for some help from a professional counselor.

The experiences of greeting either oneself or someone else may continue for as long as it helps. Sometimes we may choose to say hello again to the offender. This might be done in an unmailed letter, as I mentioned earlier, or in a guided fantasy or role play.

As we grow and heal, we learn not to take much for granted. It is important to let ourselves know that how we coped, that we survived, were miraculous, true indications of the human spirit soaring. We need to acknowledge our strengths. We also need to accept that we got through with the help of someone or something else. That human spirit might be a convenient way to look at this important quality of surviving. In a sense then, the stage of Saying Hello Again is related to Letting Go.

The theme of Hello Again signifies too that we don't need to run away, isolate ourselves, or deny some part of ourselves. We accept ourselves, and greet that whole person, building self-esteem, love, and understanding. We may say hello again to old ghosts and demons, old fears and pains, knowing we are less alone and more whole. We are integrating the old and the new, feeling safer and stronger and freer.

The Power of Reaching In and Reaching Out

Significant portions of this book have been devoted to the telling of individual stories and to commentary about them. There is great pain in the retelling of such horrors and there is discomfort in reading such words. But men need to know and to trust that the pain is valid and that the stories—our stories—are indeed true. For me to have written this book should tell you that my personal pain and shame are coming to an end.

The process of writing has been similar to the process of walking or talking: I needed support, knowledge, trust and love. I needed too a stronger sense of my abilities. I have struggled and stumbled. I have lost my way. For me, healing begins each day, sometimes at moments when I feel that I have a choice of whether to wallow or to walk, to race or renew.

As the formal writing and completing of the book was approaching an end, I was feeling joy, relief, pride, fear, and sadness. The joy is obvious; it is in celebration of completion. I was feeling relief because I had carried the burden of the stories and writing, and by sharing, it was less heavy on me. I am so proud of what this book is and hope it meets a need for each one who reads it. Yet, I was also feeling sad.

Why the sadness? This book has been a journey, a movement, a great part of my life. The book is me. As I moved toward the more final stages of writing, I could see that it was moving away from me, preparing for a public. I was having a hard time letting go. Although the book's contents are not all mine, the book is. So, I was sad for all our stories, sad that they needed to be told, and sad to let go. I know that part of anyone's healing involves a process of reaching in and reaching out.

AM I ALL BETTER? If you mean, is it all over so I don't ever have to think about it or talk about it, the answer is, 'No.' But I have come a long way. I have found ways to help me get through now. I rely on prayer and meditation. I believe that there is a God and that He does watch over me. I never have to be alone. I can pray. I never used to feel that way before. I thought and believed that I had no future because of my awful past. But I have God now.

When I seriously considered writing this book, it was the summer of 1988. I had begun my notes years before then, and I had been reading, talking, thinking, and considering it all. A clinical psychologist with whom I discussed my early awakenings to these traumas had recommended that I write. So, in 1985, I began, not thinking it would come to anything other than a personal journey. I am a curious person, so I read. I am a cautious person, so I watch. I am a brave person, so I risk. For me, that's what this phase of healing is: a time to move and to grow.

I CAN MOVE NOW. I am feeling like I can handle a problem if it should come up. I used to run away. I never stuck to the same job or the same person for very long. But I'm successful at my work. It's just that I like to move around a lot. I guess I used to run away, even from a promotion in the company. I guess I was afraid of anybody getting too close, and I didn't want anyone to know me that well. Same with friends and women. Now I feel I can move with someone or something. It's okay. I move up and down, and all around. Sometimes that means I move slowly, but I'm more comfortable now.

GETTING BETTER AND BEING BETTER are what healing is like for me. It's not all over or all gone, like a scratch or a flu-bug. What is gone is the uncertainty and the dreads. There's no cure for this mess, but there sure are good things that begin to happen. I still detest my perpetrator. The difference is, I am no longer afraid of him or other men, for that matter.

THE IMAGE OF HEALING for me is very complex. I was quiet and I was uncertain about the world. A child is innocent. Any child is. *I was innocent.* Stating those three words is so important for me.

The healing then involves a journey of self-acceptance and self-love. The healing begins when we permit ourselves to look at ourselves and see the child needing us.

WHEN I WAS BEING ABUSED . . . I would daydream about what it would be like, what life would be like, if I were stronger or more of a boy. I hated myself. And I envied and feared the more masculine-type boys, those who were self-assured, boisterous, athletic, strong. Those were the ones, I believed, who were untouched, safe and free. I didn't fit in anywhere. I saw myself as a misfit.

Now I have a better understanding of myself. I am different, and that's okay. I am learning to like and appreciate myself more. I can look in the mirror and smile at my reflection, knowing that's who I am. And what is really cool is that people close to me affirm all of this for me. I have allowed the words and feelings to come, and they love me more, not less. These are truly wonderful feelings.

Male survivors of sexual victimization have the capacity to recover and heal. We recover the young boy and we recover our self-esteem. We recover our identity and we recover ourselves. We learn to heal by reaching out for help and support and by reaching in for the gentle strength and the love we possess.

Toward a Healing of the Spirit

I struggle with the idea of spirituality, yet there have been times in my life when I experienced a "spiritual reawakening." I often find myself wondering, after such experiences, what happened to me. I think that for each of us there is a moment when we begin to trust and love ourselves with fewer conditions. Thereafter, we look for ways to help us maintain the newfound feeling of safety and goodness. We may reach the spiritual awakening stage several different ways. For example, we might use writing or drawing or dancing or praying or meditating; we might use exercise or physical conditioning; we might choose to communicate or volunteer our skills to help others.

I want to share a recent experience, one that occurred as I was working on revising and editing this manuscript. I had been writing a short piece in one of my personal journals. (In recent months I had been gathering some remnants from my childhood and adulthood to help me reach some resolution or peace over my mother's death.) The piece I was working on concerned my first time at sleep-over camp and how, apparently on my own, I formulated my definition of God.

When I moved to save the piece on my computer, it did not work. It apparently was erased by some incorrect signal I gave the computer, or so I thought. I had liked what I wrote, so I opened a file again, reconstructed and modified my essay, and pressed the correct keys to save the file. And, once more, the screen changed, discounting my request, and I again lost the essay.

I was confused and also a bit frightened that something was wrong with the computer or the disk, so I tried some different steps. I found no problem with either. The third time I approached the task I again used the same filename. Only this time, I merely recorded thoughts and key words, as if planning an outline and perhaps testing my luck. All went well, and my fragmented notes were saved.

The next day, as I was driving to see someone, tears formed in my eyes, and ever so slowly they eased down the side of my face. I began to wonder if some message was being passed on to me, that perhaps I need to explore this notion and pursue it. I felt more peaceful and serene then, and I went through my day's activities knowing that an answer would surface if I let it happen.

THE WORST WAS OVER, at least I thought or hoped so. I was nine or ten at the time, and I had survived quite a bit up to that point in my young life. I had stopped having night terrors in which I was chased by strange voices and huge shadows. I had repressed having been raped and abandoned. I had also succeeded in having had no recall of the weeks and weeks of sexual abuses of me in a foster home.

I was very quiet that summer. I had left behind me a damaged child, a violated innocence, a frightened boy, and new voices appeared, helping me to get through the days and nights. I trusted no one. There I was, a young boy with many questions and problems, and I believed that there was absolutely no one who would help me. But I also knew, from some deep sense of perception and insight, that I was attractive to people, so that I would not be left alone. Therefore, I became very careful, very hesitant, because to say or do or be the wrong thing (whatever that was) was to ask for something that was bad and harmful.

When the camp counselor sitting next to me asked me to participate in the group discussion, he had to repeat the question. My mind had drifted to some safe space in my head. "What is God, to you?" I thought about that. Having had no religious or spiritual teaching, I don't believe I knew what he meant. Yet, I began to talk, and as I spoke, the group became quiet. I said that I believed that God is everywhere in nature, in the sky, on the grass, in the wind and breeze, everywhere. The counselor who had asked me the question then held me gently against himself.

I numbed. That gentle touch of approval and support, possibly of understanding and caring, was, for me at that point in my life, too invasive, too threatening. I couldn't trust that feeling, yet I did not know why. Later when he approached me again, I stiffened, and retreated. I didn't know the differences between a good touch and a bad touch, between reserve and rejection. I only knew, from some deep and open wound, that I was not safe.

"God is everywhere," I had told them. Oh, how I had wanted to believe that. Oh, how I wish I could have trusted that wish. Yet it was a wish, and that alone might have been helpful. Although I had felt confused and hurt and abandoned, I had hope. It would take years before I could know and learn to trust that hope.

MY PERSONAL DEFINITION or description of a "higher power" is my own, developed through lots of struggle and fears. I needed to learn to trust all over again, and that has taken years. Some of us who are surviving and recovering from the pains of sexual victimizations have found comfort in organized religion; others, in other forms and types of spiritual healing and guidance. Some of us believe in one such power; others believe in many. Having searched and listened to the voices from many hearts, I think what we all share is that we are learning to trust the good power, especially the aspect which can reside in ourselves. It is that spirituality I may trust and touch any time I need or want it.

As we heal, we feel ourselves recovering a sense of who we are so that we may help reconcile our earlier losses. I am optimistic, filled with hope, so that I see opportunities for growth and change. I am less limited by other's restrictions or conditional statements.

We do not have to feel that we are almost safe or almost well or almost okay. The voices in this book say that understanding, connectedness, acceptance, and love can be ours all the time, everywhere.

It gets better, it gets worse, and it gets moving.

Several years ago, I was in a therapy group with about six or seven other adults struggling with different issues, all needing support and understanding, most offering and accepting such help. I had been having a particularly hard time dealing with my depression when suddenly I seemed to be going through a state of euphoria. The very next week I seemed to have sunk to new and lower levels of depression and sadness.

One of the group members walked me out to the parking lot. She said she thought that what I was going through was actually good. At least I was aware of where I was at that moment and what my goals could be (referring to the euphoric state I had entered). Although I am not sure I would agree that euphoria is a goal, I have always appreciated her insight about my being in a position of at least knowing where I was, where I had been, and where I might be headed.

For us who are trying to recover and heal, we reach a point where we may see that things get better and they get worse. We had been so out of touch, it feels good to awaken. We get scared and we got satiated, and it feels good to know we may retreat.

The lesson here is that we have choices. We can get better. When it feels as if things can't get worse, we know and trust ourselves (and others now) to see that we still have a future.

AS THE MEMORIES SURFACED and as I started feeling and seeing more, I was thinking why didn't I just leave well enough alone? Why didn't I just forget it all over again? It was terrible, reliving the pain, only this time it seemed even worse, like now it was in living color. But it did get better; it got easier to talk and to tell. And I got help, and that was the best (and one of the first) gifts I gave to me. Counseling with someone who understood and who was not afraid of these issues was wonderful.

The process of healing is continuous.

THIS HEALING FOR ME continues and continues. I don't see an end to it because I need to replace all those years of hurt and anger and hate and losses. Sometimes I think that I am a bottomless pit and that I keep needing to apply a medicine of sorts to keep healing.

What seems to happen for us instead is that we continue to grow. We pursue help and support through new relationships and also through new behaviors and habits. Healing involves a different way of seeing or hearing or feeling. We are becoming more alive now. For some, the arts, such as poetry or drawing or music encourage renewal. The important thing is that as the healing begins, the survivor senses life differently. Yet to promise that "everything is going to be fine" is unfair and unrealistic. There is not a day that passes that I do not know and recognize that I was used and abused as a child. One of the main differences now, as I strive to continue to recover and heal, is that I know that I am better—a better person and better for having undertaken this journey.

What's Ahead for Us?

What is survival? What's beyond it? But first, how do we get there, and once we're there, can we fall down again? We may quite understandably fear that we could fall backwards again, back into depression, anger, silence, sadness, self-inflicted pain and insult. These moments of questioning are beneficial. So often we gulped hard, made ourselves less vulnerable, more amnesic, but that was then. Now we may question. From my own experience, I know now that there will always be someone besides myself to hold me or catch me.

Many of us who have identified with a traditional male model understand a "stroke economy." Positive statements of support and recognition are doled out, as if they cost a fortune, so we grow up neither receiving nor offering them. As a survivor, I can recall that I was afraid and suspicious of anyone who would offer such statements. I questioned their intentions because I had a low self-concept and a very poor image of myself.

Some of us acquired eating disorders, becoming anorexic, malnourished, obese. We "challenged" others to comment about how we looked or acted. Some of us became addicted to substances or to people and relationships. Whatever the route, we had one thing in common: we were not taking good care of ourselves because we were not liking ourselves well enough. At some point, the burden becomes too much, and we begin to seek help and support.

But in the process of sharing, I found caring. In the process of crying, I found trying. And in the process of surviving, I found myself thriving. Like a flowering plant, I grew in all directions: outward, inward, upward, downward. I stopped running and I accepted my roots.

Self-nurturance may begin with a phone call to a friend or a therapist or a self-help group. Nurturing others may begin with stabilizing an emotionally healthy relationship or with sharing more freely and openly one's feelings. For me, an important matter was allowing myself to look at "that boy" who was betrayed and hurt and say, "Yes, that was me," and to stay with him until I would love myself. Here are some excerpts from a journal I kept:

> *I know, I know how you suffered because I was there. I couldn't help you because I was too young. I shut down a lot because that was my best defense; yet, I must let you/me know that no matter what happened, no matter what you did or felt or thought, it was okay.*
>
> *Your dreams always had a man in them, a nondescript monster (you referred to it as a monster) that chased you till*

you awoke screaming and crying. How terrifying for you . . . And all this, plus more, I'm sure, made you shut down. Do you remember how you would try to keep your face perfectly still? SO NO ONE COULD TELL WHAT YOU WERE THINKING!

But now I'm with you. I love you . . . Hopefully we will end up with one voice, affirming love for Steve . . . You're so ashamed and embarrassed that your head is spinning and you want to run and hide . . . God, it's amazing that you made it. But you did, didn't you! I love that little boy. I am sorry that we had to experience such pain and shame and confusion, but at least I understand and I can continue to work on it.

No more secrets, no more shame, no more pain, and no more victim. It was I who experienced the molestation and abuse and it was I who survived. I survived because of who and what I am. I am a good person. So, the love and acceptance and understanding I have for the quiet, lonely, needy little boy remains for the man he grew up to be: me. I love me, isn't that great!!

Secrets and shame inhabit the darkness. As victims, we existed in a world of shadows and whispers. I opened my eyes and looked up and I saw the light. When we move out of the darkness and into the light, there are new people, new relationships, new opportunities, and a new beginning.

[[9]]

Values and Biases

There are turning points for a man who is journeying through recovering and healing. Whether we begin in individual counseling, a self-help group, or in a therapy group, everyone should realize that there is no automatic trust or acceptance at the first meeting or even at the tenth meeting. No one knows for sure what pieces will be discovered, although there is the expectation that through self-discovery itself healing emerges. When there are negative or counterproductive values held by any of the people involved, walls are raised.

Each of us has values that guide us in our everyday lives. These values bias us by creating our personal range of acceptability within which we see, tolerate or reject what we or others think and do. We acquire many of our values at an early age and it is these values that help shape our later attitudes and behaviors. No one is value-free; not therapists, parents, or teachers, neither you nor I. We can, however, learn to clarify the values we hold.

Some of the value-related issues that confront us when we, as males, become victims of sexual abuse are: homophobia, non-monogamous relationships, gender identity, anger, sexuality, honesty, touch, nudity, confidentiality, anger, spirituality, trust, and truth. These are issues about which almost everyone has strong feelings and opinions. And it is these issues that surface again and again in the lives of broken boys and mending men. Some of these issues have mentioned with earlier in the book. It is particularly important for therapists, counselors and other helpers to be sensitive to these that follow.

I CANNOT RECALL A TIME when I felt more vulnerable, alone, and needy than when I was seeking help from a professional therapist. I was so scared. I felt ashamed and angry and confused. I felt like "damaged goods," unworthy and unlikeable. I was sensitive and I sought protection. I was angry and I wanted understanding.

I believe that a therapist, or any well-meaning helper, should advocate but not sermonize. A therapist may help the survivor understand what and why he (the survivor) is doing or saying something, yet it is the survivor's right to follow through on or reject these observations. This is self-empowerment for the victim/survivor so that there is authentic growth and lasting peace. This follow-through must evolve according to the victim's growth schedule, not yours.

WHEN MY THERAPIST FOUND OUT, after he and I had been working together for over six months, that I had slept around, he became furious. He called me an adulterer, and got really angry that I would be a liar (I had denied having extramarital affairs when he asked me during our first meeting) and he started preaching to me about how I was breaking a commandment.

I was floored. And then I got really scared and upset. It had taken all my courage to talk about it because I was wanting to change, and I felt like he was judging me very harshly. We continued to work together for a while but I don't think either one of us ever really trusted or liked the other again. I felt like we were going through the motions.

There are recovery approaches for victims of childhood sexual abuse which offer solace through organized religions, and for believers, this is appropriate. Prayer, meditation, channeling, counseling and hypnosis, for example, each has merits. Victims and survivors are often desperate for support and guidance. In responding to this cry for help, I may inform someone that my own spiritual program has helped me. Yet, I do not want to suggest that my program is the only way. We must all be aware of how unique we all are and not impose values that may be right for us but wrong for someone else.

> *PART OF THE HEALING PROCESS* in a group for male survivors was called spirituality, but it was based on a Judeo-Christian model, and being neither I was very uncomfortable with all this talk about God and Jesus and salvation and reading scriptures. I started feeling that I was being evaluated based on my admission or acceptance of this stuff, and I was arguing when I was really wanting to get or feel better. But I was also feeling like this brand of spirituality was their definition of healing. It was not a good experience for me. I was fighting too much. The group leader felt that I was defensive and afraid to "yield" to a higher power. That part made sense to me because power and control were such important issues to me, but it was the way it was being presented that really bothered me.

Trust and truth are issues that arise in recovery. Victims and nonvictims alike must understand that truth and trust go hand-in-hand. As we trust more, we seek and speak more truth. Truth also begets trust. Trust comes slowly, just as did the awareness and consciousness and acceptance surrounding the victimizations.

After hearing our stories in one of my workshops, one of the participants said he still was not sure why he was there. He could not believe that anything like what we had been sharing and discussing could pertain to him. Yet something in the title of the workshop or in its description called out to him. One of the other participants stayed with him, and during the course of the afternoon, each of us allowed ourselves and each other to reach a higher level of truth.

Some therapists believe that physical contact is therapeutic. For someone who had been betrayed by touch it may be a red flag. Further, survivors need to be careful not to be "seduced" by therapists who include "massage therapy" as a required part of the treatment.

> *AFTER A FEW SESSIONS*, my therapist suggested that we try massage. When I stiffened and began to protest, he tried to convince me that this was the necessary treatment because look how tense my body had become. He asked me to remove my shirt so he could examine the muscle groups. I told him to take a hike!

What helps most is the counselor or therapist who believes us and who works with us to gather the pieces, sift through, and rebuild. The issues we cover are undoubtedly related to the questions surrounding the abuses. I believe that both partners in the counseling program—victim and counselor—need to share and to accept the values each holds. It is crucial, for example, that a counselor who is homophobic recognize that this response will most assuredly interfere with the process of healing. Values clarification becomes an important element of treatment, in my estimation. The rejection of a particular set of values, or the intolerance of other sets of values, may be perceived as a rejection of the person seeking help.

Numbers

People are sometimes morbidly interested in numbers, all kinds: how many, how much, how long? It's as if to say, "Well it was only once, so what?" Or, "How come you let it go on after so many times?" Or, "Why did you let somebody else get you? Didn't you learn your lesson?"

IN 1968, I VISITED an exhibit at the Montreal Expo which was commemorating the victims of the Nazi Holocaust. Approximately twelve million people had been killed, half that number because the Nazis hated Jewish blood, the other half because of racial, political, or sexual inferiority. Twelve million lives were snuffed out.

The most startling part of that exhibit however was not the photographs of bodies that had once been alive and lively now piled in trains, in lines, in trenches, in camps. No, the most poignant and the most upsetting (for me, and I assume for other late-witnesses) was the sight of a pair of little shoes whose owner had not even been allowed to outgrow. That one pair of shoes did it for me. I saw that little child though no photograph or records could confirm that child's real identity; that child has remained an image for me, the shoes being the sign.

I don't have a pair of shoes to let you see how young I was when I was sexually molested. You probably would look down at my feet now and say, see you're a big boy now, grow up.

In the numbers game some people want to predict outcomes, to think and talk in terms of cause and effect. For example, some studies report that over 80 percent of gay men were sexually abused as children.[3] So there is the argument that sexual abuse causes homosexuality. I have trouble understanding how anyone would conclude that overpowering or betraying a youngster will cause that youngster to grow up to relate strongly and positively to men. As the accounts of victims confirm over and over again, the sex crimes against boys are not primarily sexual, in the sense of sexuality understood by adult nonvictims. These were physical crimes committed to exert pressure and to assert power.

While it is accurate to assume that we, like hostages in an aircraft hijacking, might have identified in some way with the offender, we have not "chosen" a preference or orientation for sexual loving because of that original crime. If we had, and since one out of six males has been sexually victimized as boys, then the incidence of gay men would be significantly greater than the consistently reported ten percent.[4]

Some experts look at the alarming reports that perpetrators who are caught disclose that they too had been sexually abused as young boys.[5] So in the minds of some, the implication is that a victim will become a criminal. That is a frightening legacy and not substantiated by any careful studies of adults who were the victims of childhood sexual abuse. Since the subject of male sexual victimization has been taboo until recently, little research has been addressed to finding out what happens to victims during their

---

[3] Both the *The Spada Report* (1979) and *The Hite Report on Male Sexuality* (1981) give reference to such incidences. The high incidences are also cited by Porter (1986). Further, a study by Johnson and Shrier (1987) found that 8 of 11 male adolescents who reported having been molested by males identified themselves as homosexual.

[4] See discussion in footnote number 1, page vii.

[5] For example, Blount and Chandler (1979) found evidence of abuse in 8 of 15 adolescent male psychiatric patients who themselves evidenced assaultive behavior. Swift (1979) also cites evidence that a large proportion of males who abuse children sexually were sexually victimized themselves as boys. Porter (1986) echoes this disturbing finding.

adult years. We may know something about criminals who get caught, but we know very little about the victims who comprise the "silent majority."

Reports of sexual victimizations against males by males often label the offender as homosexual. This has the effect of tarring the victim with the same brush as the criminal. It is much worse than guilt by association. It is guilt by innocence. Consider the term "homosexual rape" as it is used to describe such victimizations in prisons, for example. The victim is said to be selected as victim because he is weaker, younger, softer.

Although the sexual victimization of males by males has been perceived as homosexual, the only way it could be categorized as such is that it involves people of the same sex. It is more accurate to term it "same-sex" sexual victimization. As we have learned from the sexual assault of females by males, rape, the crime is motivated by power, not sex. It is a crime in which one who is more in power and control chooses to use parts of his body against another person.

Some numbers are astonishing. One in six males has been sexually assaulted during his childhood.[6] (Some say the figure might be as many as one in four.)[7] Very few offenders are caught, and of that small number, only a small percentage is convicted. Offenders reportedly have sexually victimized scores of children before they are caught.[8] So, many of us have been victims of the same offender.

---

[6] See footnote number 1, page vii.

[7] See footnote number 1, page vii.

[8] Personal communication. Lynn McCarthy, Counselor, Rhode Island Rape Crisis Center.

Touching as an Issue: "Handle with Caring"

During the past few years, many people's level of consciousness and awareness about different kinds of touching, especially
children's, has greatly increased. There are now books on sexual
abuse and programs for school children, offered through local
rape crisis centers, that teach prevention. Through these means,
children may become safer and freer. The sad fact is, however,
that not enough children are reached soon enough.

It would be so easy to "just say no," but that is not enough. It
is not enough because perpetrators and offenders need to be the
ones to say no also: no to their power games and to their control;
no to their disregard of the fragile human condition. For those of
us who had experienced sexual victimization as boys, the issue of
touch remains critical.

HUGGING IS THE NEW THING. Everybody wants to
hug everybody. But not me. I go to places where there's
everybody hugging me and I can hardly stand it. But I still
have trouble telling someone I don't want that.

We were all sitting in a circle in a workshop for male
survivors of sexual abuse in boyhood and the subject of
touching came up. It was like someone had opened a really
old and deep wound. We all agreed that this was something
we wanted to explore as a topic that morning. I did not want
any group hug afterwards. I did not want anyone coming up
to me and hugging me and holding me against his body. I
don't care what anyone's intentions are because I hate that.

This was one of the first times we could voice our
concerns and not feel we were going to hurt anybody's
feelings. Even if I hurt someone's feelings because I do not
want them to touch me, it's okay. I need that kind of control
over my body right now. Ask my permission. Let me define
the limits for you. I never could before.

One thing that becomes clearer, and therefore more helpful to our understanding of the effects of our childhood sexual victimization, is that before recovery can proceed we must explore how some fundamental internal circuits might have been switched. Over and over we hear testimony to how many of us "numbed out," how we seemed to have lost a part of our physical being.

As our sexuality and as our sensuality emerged and coursed toward development and growth, we became confused and afraid. Often, the physical aspects of the assaults affect our expectations for physical intimacy and sexual expressiveness. Some of us became "great performers," pleasing our partners to some lofty level of ecstacy perhaps. Others of us became "hedonists," selfish for our own pleasures and gratification.

We may confuse pain for pleasure, sex for love, touch for intimacy, physical contact for physical threat, ourselves for others and others for ourselves, someone else for the perpetrators, and ourselves for them. A single touch may sear us and reopen a wound. We may work to avoid that or we may try to relive it, hoping this time it will be different.

Until we are more aware and better supported and accepted, until we are acknowledged and respected, we may find ourselves increasingly alienated from ourselves and others. The anaesthesia of sexual assault needs help in being treated. Unlike novocaine, it does not wear off on its own. It is too deep and too base.

I HAVE THESE TWO VOICES in my head. One says that I love to be touched and fondled and I enjoy it. But the other makes me feel guilty and dirty for accepting and enjoying it. I still get confused about the differences between the attention I receive now and the attention I once received that was pleasurable but wrong. I have a lot of guilt over that because I never felt violated or abused. He made me feel good. He got off on that. I also know that he used bribes with me. And he was pushing for more from me. But at ten, I was loving it, even with all the confusion over secrecy. So now I have to deal with that too, and it's hard.

We may be touched on different levels: physically, yes, and also emotionally, by the sound of another's voice, the look in their eyes, the way they are sitting. A survivor needs to understand this and appreciate the differences and boundaries. Sometimes, I want to be held but not touched. I need to know that about myself and what it is that you wish and need.

Sometimes the survivor goes through a stage when touch is not an issue at all. At other times, it is a looming issue. As we gain self-empowerment and self-acceptance, we are better able to understand and to share the boundaries that once, and for a long time, we did not know.

⟦ 10 ⟧

CHAPTER

How Could This Happen?

The topic of sexual victimization of boys is still met with reactions such as "unbelievable" or "how could this happen?" All of us have had those thoughts too. For survivors, there is an echo from the past demanding to know why no one came forward, why there was no witness, no help.

For Parents and Professionals, Attention Please!

What do you do upon hearing a disclosure of sexual abuse? How do you help the boy to trust once again and to talk? Let us begin by reviewing how a boy is brought into a sexually abusive relationship and how he is kept there.

I WAS VERY LONELY. I spent a lot of time by myself. I never felt like the other boys, I didn't like to fight and wrestle or anything like that. Most of all though I missed my father. He was never around.

My brother and I were left alone for long periods of time. Our parents left me in his care when he was fourteen and I was eight. That's when it began.

So, there is first of all the loneliness. Then there might be a lack of adequate and appropriate supervision.

NO ONE EVER PAID SO MUCH ATTENTION TO ME. I mean, he was really interested in my hobbies. It was easy for him to get into my room because that's where my models were. He was like a big brother, and nobody paid any attention. So when he started, I accepted it as part of the deal.

In addition, the lack of understanding about the differences between homosexual orientation and preference, on the one hand, and homophobic responses to situations and experiences that may occur between two males, has produced fears, shame, and silence.

WHEN YOU'RE FOURTEEN there's no way you're saying that happened to you. That would be it. Everybody's calling you a fag. For my parents, especially my father, that's the worse. So I let it continue. I was too scared to tell because then he would say that I really am a faggot.

The victim is blamed. He should have known better or he should have fought more or run faster. There is the view, unfortunately still held by people, that eyes the victim with some degree of doubt and suspicion. Perhaps he wanted it to happen. He probably was just as much to blame for it.

"YOU DON'T MEAN YOU LET HIM DO THAT! Goddamn, what's wrong with you?" Enough said? You think I was ever gonna tell anyone else?

Boys who are "tutored" by older males with explicit sex are targets for more involved and intimate contacts. An open approach at home to sexuality and to responsibilities associated with sexuality would indicate to the boy who his reliable sources are. When sex is defined as something "only a real man can do," then the mystique of masculinity might invite the boy to grow too fast and unprotected.

I WASN'T DOING ANYTHING WRONG. He was the faggot. I just let him do me. And it was pretty good. I even got him to pay me . . . But later it was hard on me because I kept doing it and he got me to let other men touch me. And when I was fifteen, I was hustling for real.

In a recent column, Ann Landers was told by a counselor that it is important to ask if a person had been sexually abused as a child. Otherwise, depression or anger could be treated as a symptom of something very different and very far from the real problem. My advice is when you suspect, ask. Give unconditional love and support, and ask again. Invite a boy's trust and candor by being open and accepting yourself.

Often a boy's references to sexual abuse are oblique and indirect because he senses that sexual victimization is an unmentionable in his home or school. A parent or professional should be sensitive to clues revealed in the boy's language. These are a some words that reflect confused, ambivalent, and ambiguous messages for male victims:

zipper; down there; I don't remember; I don't want to talk about it; but nothing really happened; he didn't mean it; he said not to tell; i can't tell you; how do you know he can't get me? but he'll find out; but he'll know it was me who said; what's going to happen to me? what will happen to him? it doesn't hurt; then it's true what they say about me; but he's my friend; but he's my father; but he's special; he said he'll stop; but he said it's okay for us; where is he now? i don't lie.

Witness: Is There No One?

I once was shown a picture drawn by an incest victim in which she was on the couch with her father while the rest of her family, including her mother and two siblings, sat in the living room watching TV. The young woman who had drawn the picture did not portray herself watching the TV. Instead, she was performing fellatio.

I looked at that picture, trying to take it all in, not to take it in, wanting to make him stop, to make her stop and escape that awful place. And then I wanted to scream and yell and wake all those TV-zombies and say, "Look! Where were they while her father was making her his pleasure?" Why did they not know or see the changes in her?

MY SISTER MARRIED a guy who beat her up, so she divorced him, but before it was over she was left with two kids. She got married again, and things seemed fine. I was really happy for her because we didn't have it so great as kids. Our father was a drunk, and he used to get violent. I never told anybody but he used to get me in the middle of the night. My mother would be crying in their room and he would be sniffing how sorry he was and he would find his way to my room. It started out innocent, me helping him get comfortable, but soon he was sobering up or something, and he would get me.

Well, this one night my phone rings, and it's my sister, and she's sobbing because she just found out that her second husband was molesting her two kids who are now ten and twelve, and I ran over to their house and I was shaking so bad as I watched my niece and nephew sobbing on the sofa, I told my sister. I told her everything. And I was feeling so rotten because I should have been able to tell what was going on in their lives, and then she gets real quiet and says that she had known about our father, that she had heard him with me. He never touched her because the one time he tried she was filing her nails and she stabbed him in the hand.

What a mess this is. We're all trying to get better. We're in counseling together. I am still amazed that she knew. I don't know if my mother did.

Boys, more than girls, are encouraged to explore and to go farther away from home. It appears that they are less of a concern for parents than girls. This lowered surveillance, coupled with the perpetrator often being someone known by the family, makes it fairly easy to separate a victim from the crowd. Sometimes special circumstances, such as disrupted families, place children at risk.

I WAS IN A FOSTER HOME for a while. The daughter of the guy who ran the foster home used to follow me around. It was like she was following me from a distance. The image I have of her is that she would have this half-grin on her face, and she called me "sissy." As I go over all this in my head, several things occur to me. One is that she knew that her father was now molesting me. I think she was both relieved and resentful. He was paying a lot of attention to his "new charge" and he was taking plenty from me. I also feel that she might have been confused because now he was taking a boy. I was so fragile then, so alone, so in need of attention and love. I cried a lot, and I think too that she knew that and she called me a sissy because of that.

For the professionals who work with children, there is much that may be done to help at every stage——before, in a preventive way, and during or after, by recognizing symptoms and behavior patterns. There is always the need for advocacy. Once again, an open and honest approach in communicating is essential. Teachers, counselors, therapists, and medical personnel all can help.

First, be knowledgeable. Also, be sensitive, aware, and even somewhat suspicious. A significant percentage of boys will have been sexually victimized by their sixteenth birthdays.[9] This is not a statement meant to create panic. It is made to emphasize the extent of the problem. One boy in six faces this pain. This one boy in six will probably seek solace in substance abuse or other offenses against himself or others because he has not known how else to express himself over this devastation. This one boy in six is probably going to believe that his sexuality is questionable. He may try to pursue a life without understanding himself, thereby creating more self-hate and an incomplete existence.

People whose professions bring them into personal contact with boys must know how to recognize symptoms of abuse and how to help a boy who may be troubled by sexual victimization. It is no longer acceptable to ignore the realities and potential threats. Do not suppress something because it is uncomfortable or unpleasant to you.

I WAS BEING SEEN by a child psychiatrist because I had been having night terrors. I can still recall how he dismissed my manipulating two doll figures (one adult male, the other a boy) by telling me to "put all the people together at the dinner table." I obeyed, learning to suppress further the conflicts I was feeling about being forced to have oral sex with a close friend of the family.

The adults involved with the young need to be aware of shifts in behaviors and changes in attitudes because these can be an indicator of trouble. Sudden changes in a child's general mood and outlook are a clear warning. Often, the boy-victim lacks the ability or willingness to describe in words what is happening, so he changes how he acts.

---

[9] Based on the retrospective reports in the literature and on predictions from law enforcement agencies, it can be assumed that this is an accurate statement. See also, footnote number 1, page vii. Porter (1986) also provides evidence.

MY MOTHER used to dismiss my sullenness and my outbursts of anger as "going through a phase." Sure, some phase. I guess I thought that what I was feeling and what I was thinking were mine alone, so I never opened to anyone. And nobody seemed to care that much, just figuring well, here comes another John Wayne type. And you know what? I hated John Wayne. He was always so forceful, and he hardly ever talked. There were no positive male role-models when I was growing up, trying to endure and escape the pain. There were no people around who would listen to me not talk. So I just figured I was waiting to grow up, to outgrow this mess, and go somewhere no one would know. Funny, that's practically where I was anyway. Nobody knew. Except the man, and vaguely, me.

I REMEMBER there was this one male teacher in my elementary school who tried to reach me, and although I did not disclose to him, I am grateful to his attempts. I don't think he knew or even considered that I had been sexually abused. But he saw this troubled little boy who was having headaches every day and he tried to talk to him. But I was so scared, so distrustful, that I clammed up. But he did try, he just didn't have the right vocabulary. Perhaps too he did not have the right suspicions. He kept using his daughter as a comparison (because of our similar ages), and I was not hearing him after that. I mean, if being "girlish" got me into this mess, why did I want to align myself with her? But he did try. I still remember his name.

We all need to be aware of changes in a child's general looks, affect, and behaviors which may be clues to sexual abuse. The following is a listing of symptoms compiled by Barbara Walsh and Elda Dawber, Rhode Island Department for Children and Their Families (made available through *R.I.Rape Crisis Center Counselor-Advocate Training Program*, Judy Kinzel, Director of Volunteers). Please note that I have adapted the list for males:

In younger boys, we are alerted to the possibility of sexual abuse when there is:

- venereal disease;
- venereal warts;
- herpes;
- frequent unexplained sore throats;
- intense, fearful reactions to adult males;
- nightmares and other sleep disturbances;
- early sexualized behavior, such as excessive or compulsive masturbation;
- sexualized kissing or thrusting;
- attempts to involve others in sexual activity;
- persistent and inappropriate sexual play with peers or toys;
- excessive sexual curiosity;
- explicit sexual knowledge (behavior and knowledge unusual for the young age);
- hints about sexual activity.

More subtle or equivocal indicators of possible sexual abuse are:

- bed or pants wetting or soiling;
- unexplained gagging;
- depression;
- becoming very shy;
- self-absorbed;
- rocking constantly;
- poor self-image;
- excessive swearing;
- fear of the dark or of staying in the room with the door closed;
- sudden drop in school achievement;
- arriving at school early and leaving late;

- running away;
- aggressiveness with peers and/or younger children;
- compliance or overconformity;
- pseudomature behavior;
- gender-role confusion; and,
- physically "seductive" and overly friendly (jumping onto lap, grasping leg or waist).

Elda Dawber and Barbara Walsh of the *Rhode Island Department for Children and Their Families* report that combinations of signs and symptoms from the preceding lists are also present in the adolescent, with these possible additions: engaging in self-destructive and delinquent behavior, such as chemical or substance abuse; self-mutilation; and, suicidal gestures/attempts/ideation. Further, the adolescent male victim may have somatic complaints such as infection, abdominal pain, headaches, or muscle aches. He also may have an eating disorder: anorexia, bulimia, overeating, sudden weight loss or gain; indiscriminate sexual activity, prostitution, or asexuality. He also may have become the regular recipient of gifts from a man. Also present might be intense sibling rivalry, conflict with one parent (the nonperpetrator), and complaints of confusion.

The professional working with children and adolescents needs to note family dynamics, such as:

- a father or stepfather who never attends a meeting or conference (when requested) and who will not remain in the same room with a counselor or other child advocate;
- a family working hard to keep secrets; or,
- role confusions whereby the child assumes parental responsibilities.

Walsh and Dawber warn that the offending parent often "sides with" the child and is very possessive and jealous, wanting to be alone with the child-victim. On the other hand, the child may be afraid to be alone with him. It has been observed that the two——victim and perpetrator——sometimes appear to be "buddies". The father may be very concerned about the boy's bodily changes.

Most of us have believed that it is the stranger who stalks little boys from behind the bushes, kidnaps them and molests them. These are the kinds of cases that are reported and sensationalized in the media. They do occur. But, like other sex crimes such as date rape and father-daughter incest, sexual victimization of boys is underreported.

The perpetrator typically knows the boy and he knows about him. The boy is probably not his first victim, and unless he is stopped, the boy will not be his last victim. Fathers, uncles, older brothers and teachers, counselors and members of the clergy have all been reported as perpetrators. Most often, he was someone to whom we looked up, someone we trusted and admired, as did our family and community.

The perpetrator seeks a boy who is in some state of need, whether it is for companionship, attention, warmth, or material items. Most of the time, he is looking for a victim who is already afraid or isolated or insecure, a boy from a dysfunctional family system in which communication is not open.

So, as difficult as it may seem, it is critical that we prepare our children. Boys need to be counseled and advised. Boys need to know that it is always all right to tell if they think or feel something is wrong. Further, this requires that parents talk about the subject of child sexual abuse. One enlightened approach to this is contained in the Boy Scouts of America's *Cub Scout Handbook*, where a "Parent's Guide" offers information about sexual and substance abuse.

Creating a stable environment in which communication is encouraged, where there is mutual respect, and where everyone is taken seriously, helps to provide adequate protection and care. Boys need support and understanding, and this is most easily accomplished by open communication. Boys can feel pressured to assume a traditional male sex role, and without discussion of responsibility and limitations, they may be easy targets for sexual victimization.

A few years ago, I met a woman whose son had been molested by a family friend living across the street. The boy disclosed the abuses after his father picked up on some age-inappropriate language and concerns when his father was toweling off from a shower. There were tears and retractions. There were denials and accusations. Yet throughout the ordeal, the parents stood by their son and gave him love, support and understanding. When the neighbor accused the boy (age seven) of being the culprit because of "homosexual tendencies," and word spread through the neighborhood, the family weathered the storm.

I, The Author

I had thought this was all over now. Counseling, group discussions, readings, sharing, were all part of what was supposed to help me face the monsters and go on with my life. All that happened, up to a point. Now I live with the memory trace, with the ghosts who still come out to haunt me.

I see being a survivor as involving hurting, hiding, and healing. Yet I could not have known the extent of this journey toward recovery and integration. I did not realize that, from time to time, I would still hurt, that I would want or need to hide, and that the healing would not feel very good or gentle all the time. My poetry helps me. Each poem speaks of me, to me, and I need to be more honest and let them come.

I know better now that the question of why these memories and associations emerge is not half as significant as how they keep interfering if I am not careful, aware and in touch with myself. It is when I realize that I can protect myself from the hurt, not by hiding, but by standing fast and holding on that I see myself as okay. But all that takes time. I think what happens to me is that either I am all-consumed with the hurt and the anger and the shame or I am numbed by the denial and the withdrawal and the amnesia.

I notice that there are many ways that I hurt myself, by putting myself down, for example. Overeating is one of the most powerful ways I have to act on myself because I do not like myself when I am heavy; nor do I find myself attractive.

There is something else. As I reread portions of my journals, I become aware of how fragile I am. I am still grieving, and I think this grieving will continue throughout my life because I still seem to discover the losses. I don't mean to think about these things; they just seem to come to me. I am amazed by the intricate nature of surviving.

Each step in preparing and in writing this book has involved fears and self-doubts. For example, when I received the letter from the publisher, responding to my materials, I convinced myself that I was being rejected. I was afraid to open the letter, and I created, or recreated, times of disappointment and failure, denying myself the opportunity to face honestly the current reality.

Consider the young boy who has been hurt and betrayed. He will not think that it is the older male who is wrong; he will internalize, holding it in for as long as he can. Perhaps the perpetrator was an alcoholic. Perhaps he was a man living alone or one who portrayed himself as lonely. Perhaps he was our father who had made many different demands on us. How were we to know that this time would be different, more difficult, most devastating. Yet, we blamed ourselves. We didn't deserve anything different. We did not know that there was anything different to be offered to us.

The anger is not gone, no. And I suppose that, although in the arms of a supportive group experience I thought it was all behind me, I am not quite ready to forgive. And I think I fear that if I do forgive, it will mean that I forgot. And since I was in a state of numbness and amnesia for so long (most of my life), I am not willing to entertain such a loss. No, I do not want to forget; I do not want to forgive. And yet, I know that means that I am not through forgiving myself. What will it take?

I am not sure. But I do realize that I have not finished forgiving myself for having been the victim. Odd, I don't think twice in other people's cases, but I tend to be hard on myself. Is it that for so long I internalized everything and everyone? Is it that I still feel that I do not have the power and control to exorcise these demons? And at times, they are still hurting me so much. I can feel them still. I can hear them and I can smell them. But what about me? Do I yet dare allow myself to feel and hear and smell myself? Do I allow myself to complete the fantasy in the safety and privacy of myself? I have certainly made attempts over the years, and this progress of course continues.

Individual and group counseling helped. However, as the stresses, demands, and strains increase in my work, I find myself vulnerable. I am open to criticism, for example. And I am open to getting run-down physically. And when I ought to be caring for myself more, with proper diet and exercise, for example, it is then that I do not nurture myself. I need to give myself permission to be human. I need to give that little boy inside me permission to be human, to feel and cry and accept and love. And I need to feel him, accept him, and to love him myself.

So, again my thoughts turn to poems that remain incomplete. There's a message for me, I know. I recorded *last rose* recently and I'm not sure that it's done; nor do I think I understand it very much at all, probably because it's not done. I'm trying to stay with these ideas and feelings since I seem to do better when I begin with metaphorical language. I know that my rose garden has become more important to me. When I saw and then brought in the rosebud from late October, saving it from the first frost, it was very important for me to have done all this.

I feel comforted and serene when I garden, and my rose garden is a site that I especially enjoy visiting. As I worked on my own garden, the image of an old Japanese man became a part of me, so that I could see him and I could feel his presence as I moved the stones and pebbles. I accept him and that image, although even now I do not quite understand the significance of any of it. (That image of the old Japanese man is interesting to me. He seems to serve as spiritual partner. I am not sure why, but I do know that I have always been comforted and nurtured by Japanese culture and art, especially.) I do know that I felt safe and sure and very much at peace. I accept all that for now even though it does make me uncomfortable not to understand something about myself!

Survivors and victims of sexual crimes understand each other. Once there is the admission that it happened, and once we acknowledge with others that it happened to us, we begin to reconnect. This is a complex process, as I find that one thing leads to another. Then I go to something else or I abandon it for a while, returning if and when I feel that I can.

I revisit old times, even now. For example, I have just recently begun to put together more about my foster home experiences. I have felt safer to acknowledge some of the pleasure, realizing too the intense pain I then felt by having been abandoned. I remember that by the time "he" came along, I was ready in terms of my confused and empty or needy state. He was rougher because I was a little older then and because I probably threatened his sense of what masculine was. By forcing me to "take" him, his responsibility was minimal as was his involvement. He was in charge. By trying to make me swallow, he wished to hide the evidence. I vomited on him immediately after, and he was angry. He was also frightened. Little did he know how long I would hold his secret.

It's not so easy telling my story though, and it's not such a relief. True, with time, I do feel better and it does get easier, but I still resent the time spent and the time lost over this issue. To have been a child-victim was hell. To have been used as a receptacle when I expected and needed human warmth and human contact was criminal. So here I am now trying to explain and trying to understand myself. Yes, myself, as I was molded and manipulated. I still am angry.

The anger remains a potent issue with which all survivors must deal. We find ways to be constructive and creative with that old anger. Otherwise, it may turn to rage—against ourselves as well as others.

What else do I need to understand? How I accept love and loving is something I continue to discover. At other times I appear to be fearful of allowing myself to revel in pleasure. I have grown less detached, and I am able to share better, so that I do not have to be in control. Yet I know that it was those times when I had no control, when it was I who was under the power and influence of someone stronger than I, that I was detached. That is probably how I survived. I served out others' fantasies, so I created my own.

I now know what happened to me in the foster home. It becomes clearer as I allow myself to push away the ghouls and to knock down the webs that have for too long prevented me from knowing the truth. Certainly I have been able to recall how Mr. G. bathed me and fondled me. But for so long the images stopped there, so that I saw a blackout, mostly my own. Sometimes, I would associate this with a great shadow above me. I have learned that the shadow was that of him lowering himself on me, covering, smothering, using me.

I do not think that we "outgrow" the pain. Understanding it and not letting it run one's life . . . perhaps yes. The scars remain. As a survivor, I know they remain. What one decides to do with the scars is of course an individual matter. I may let go, but there will always be the residue on me and inside me.

It was as an adult that I was able to feel safer and more secure so I could disclose even a bit of the experience of the aftermath of sexual abuse. Once I was shattered, scared that my world was falling apart, that I had misrepresented myself to my partner, that I was "damaged goods" and that my sexuality was not even real. This was very difficult. Even now, I have those moments when I am caught off guard, when I am frightened or threatened by what could only be the remotest possibility, that I am still vulnerable to attack. And then I close down, which of course creates that previous isolation I had suffered.

There have been turning points in my life, which signaled some level of consciousness, and for that moment, it was all I could tolerate. There was the film, *Private Sessions*. It was a scene with the young girl on the stairs that evoked a long-hidden scene in my own life. In each case, those stairs brought an adult to our bedroom.

I know too that my emerging spirituality offers me peace and stability because it fosters self-awareness and self-growth. I am not religious, yet I recognize the potential of a higher power (not necessarily one). I recall that when I was asked as a child about my thoughts on God, I remarked that it was nature, all around us. I feel that still, and it comforts me. Now I look inside myself because I am learning to trust and to love myself. I am worthy. What a revelation, in contrast to what and how I had been made to feel as a child, abused and abandoned, betrayed. That is part of the broken boy. I needed to mend us.

As I grew, I think I tried to pull in everything and hold a lot inside myself. Of course, I was not able to accomplish all that, so I cracked at various times and in various places inside, so that I became a shattered man. I could not contain it all, especially not on my own. I was frightened and I was angry. As a child, I was quiet, practically withdrawn. As an adult, I developed strategies to turn that inwardness out, so that I could strike out in anger or in spite. Then, I would retreat. Each time I went through that, it hurt, and I disintegrated a little more each time. In interpersonal relationships, except for the closest friendships I have had, I felt I had to be in control at all times. After such outbursts however, it would be harder to go back to the way things had been. I would feel the need to retreat further, moving away from genuine sharing.

The cycle slows, it is broken and changed. What I needed was to trust and accept myself for who I am at this moment, recogniz-

ing the past and my potential. For a survivor of sexual victimization, this is difficult because to a male, sex is power. If a boy is
assaulted, he may believe that his way out of this cycle is to
become stronger and overpower others.

There is an additional issue: forgiveness. Some will say that
when we finally forgive ourselves, we will forgive others. That is
not a good argument. While it is true that we may need to forgive
ourselves even though we are not to blame, it does not follow that
we need to forgive *someone who is to blame*. And perhaps for
some people that works. For me, it does not. I think that I
associate forgiving with forgetting, and I will not do that since the
early losses of certain memories contributed to some of my
problems. Forgive? No. Some of us choose not to forgive because
although society will label us survivors, the world needs to
acknowledge that above all we were victims.

As I continue this journey, I think more about the broken boy
(me) and the shattered man (also me), and I can trace more, in
better detail the hurting and the hiding and the healing. It is a
continuing process. And when it gets too bad or too hurtful to
remember, I may hide until I can heal some more. We just don't,
as one friend of mine once suggested to me, "get over it," as if we
are talking about the common cold.

I used to have the most awful night terrors, awakening in the
middle of the night screaming and sobbing and trembling.
Someone was chasing me, an evil man, and he was going to hurt
me . . .. Then I would forget the rest of the dream and not want
to talk about it anymore. Even in my sleep, even in the safety of
my own bedroom, I was afraid that once more he would get me.
Well, he did. Each time I fell asleep, there he was. After awhile,
the dreams stopped. But I remember as an adult having that same
dream, and waking up, unable to catch my breath, sweating,
shivering, trembling, hyperventilating. Over and over again. I never
could see his face.

When I first remembered the painful realities of my childhood, I was an adult less than two months away from my fortieth birthday. It was then that I remembered and was certain about what had happened to me. During the initial phases of my recovery, I chose not to look closely at much of anything. It was only later, having felt safer with the help of a sensitive and competent counselor, that I began to let go of the terrors I felt. I began to look the monsters and the ghosts right in the eye. My writing this is an example of my continuing to work to let go, not in the sense of releasing to be rid of something, but in the way we may release a balloon and let it rise above us, freely and without many limits. I let go, and the pain grows both stronger and weaker. At first, the pain is hideous in its strength and potency. It feels cold and miserable. Then it weakens because I don't work to hold it back anymore; I let it go. I am open to more of what life may offer.

Sometimes that has been frightening because I lack the ability to know, to predict. I see that I have potential and I recognize that there is a lot more to me than I used to think. I am a good person, with good motives. Part of my recovery process has been to say good-bye, to bid farewell to old destructive relationships, people, places, habits, things. I had held on, and it was time to let go. Holding on was part of the victim mind-set.

Recovery is continuous. I realize that I need to pursue and retreat several times, and it is that risk-taking and that retreating that creates a balance for me. More and more memories and associations emerge and I discover and know more about myself. That takes time. It is so much more convenient to deny the ambivalence of both the here-and-now and of the past: I see myself as a participant, whether willing or not, consenting or not, aware or not, and I may chastise myself.

I mentioned before that I was also afraid of my own maleness. Adolescence was a painful time for me. I felt inadequate physically, and I continued to be victimized because I could never measure up. The tender, gentle, sensitive side of me, which was attractive to some and which was positive for me at the same time, was a detriment. I remember my mother telling me that a man could change tires and grow flowers, an attempt, I think, to help me accept the "other" side of myself. But this ended up confusing me because I didn't want to change tires and I was still afraid to grow flowers.

I grew up feeling there was something strange and different about myself, getting vibes from older males that I was a disappointment, a shame. I was not treated well by them, and although I did not remember the earlier assaults against me, I knew enough to steer clear of them.

I wouldn't cry. No matter what was done to me, I refused to let on that I felt anything. Nothing! I held a lot inside and I survived by keeping to myself, not letting anyone in. Why should I? When I did, it hurt me. I rarely talked, and I trusted adults even less than peers. I was quiet, withdrawn, lonely: the perfect target for a perpetrator.

If you let me talk, I can go on for days and days. I will tell you everything, even what you don't want to know. I remember reading Ralph Ellison's book, *Invisible Man*, and I thought: that's me. Nobody sees me because they don't want to be bothered. I don't exist. Well, I do! I did back then too.

When I first discovered that I had been raped as a child, I was an adult, and I was devastated. I needed to talk about it, about me, and it was hard getting many people to listen and understand. It was like what coming out must be for a gay person, except I was so ashamed. People's reactions sometimes made me wish I had kept quiet. I did a lot of retreating back then. I still do. I'm not completely out because I still feel the shame, like a shadow.

What's the whole story? Will I ever know it all? Is it possible not to know all the details and get on with it? I think so. It is with hope that this book was conceived and written, and it is with hope that it is given.

Epilogue

Several years ago, I proposed to the *National Organization for Changing Men (NOCM)* that I lead a workshop at our national conference in St. Louis for male survivors of sexual victimization. I suggested this because I wanted to connect with other men who had shared this experience. At the time, I was in the initial stages of recovering and healing, so I saw my action as an attempt at self-help too. NOCM is a profeminist, gay-affirmative, male-positive organization to which I have belonged. So although I was anxious and apprehensive about this whole issue, I was feeling fairly safe in making such an offering. The workshop proposal was accepted and it was scheduled for a ninety-minute (standard) session. I was prepared (overly, I would say) with many activities and the chalkboards in the room (a classroom at Washington University) were filled with ideas and notes, some of which had been taken from a book by Gil, *Outgrowing the Pain.*

Four of us showed. Within that room, we somehow managed to transcend the physical set-up of the seats, so for the next two-and-a-half hours, we rode it out. I used that wording because I remember feeling as if we were in a small boat in the midst of a terrible sea-storm, holding on to each other's shoulders and arms and, most important, each other's words. We lifted and supported each other in a way that none of us had experienced before. We became a Circle of Four, and to this day I feel that bond, unbroken, strengthened. I was less afraid. I am less afraid still.

I have offered workshops since the one in St. Louis, and I am reaffirmed, as I believe each of is, as we listen, feel, and share some part of ourselves. In 1988, at the thirteenth National Conference on Men and Masculinity, sponsored by *NOCM*, in Seattle, I offered such a workshop for male survivors of childhood sexual victimization, calling it *"One in six . . . "* to show the estimated number of males who have been sexually victimized. By then, I had read more, thought and felt more, and I was talking and examining more. I was feeling better yet sadder, better because of my own personal journey, sadder because too many of us were still victims.

I walked to the building on the Seattle University campus, where the workshop was scheduled, and when I entered the room I was not fully prepared for what I saw. The room was filled.

Selected References

Anthony, E. James and George H. Pollock (eds.), *Parental Influences in Health and Disease*. Boston: Little, Brown and Company (1985).

Anthony, E. James and Bertram J. Cohler (eds.), *The Invulnerable Child*. New York: Guilford Press (1987).

Armstrong, Louise, *Solomon Says: A Speakout on Foster Care*. New York: Pocket Books (1989).

Bass, Ellen and Marti Betz, *I Like You to Make Jokes with Me, But I Don't Want You to Touch Me*. Chapel Hill: Lollipop Power (1981).

Black, Claudia and Laurie Zagon, *"It's Never Too Late to Have a Happy Childhood": Inspirations for Adult Children*. New York: Ballantine (1989).

Blanchard, Geral, Male victims of child sexual abuse: A portent of things to come. *Journal of Independent Social Work*, 1986, 1, 19-27.

Blount, Hal R. and Theodore Chandler, Relationship between child abuse and assaultive behavior in adolescent male psychiatric patients. *Psychological Reports*, 44, 1126.

Bolton, Frank, Larry Morris and Ann MacEachron, *Males At Risk: The other side of child sexual abuse*. Newbury Park, CA: Sage (1989).

Broussard, Sylvia D. and William G. Wagner, Child sexual abuse: Who is to blame? *Child Abuse and Neglect*, 1988, 563-569.

Bruckner, Debra F. and Peter E. Johnson, Treatment of adult male victims of childhood sexual abuse. *Social Casework*, 1987, 68, 81-87.

Butler, Francelia and Richard Rotert (eds.), Triumphs of the Spirit in Children's Literature. Hamden, CT: *Library Professional Publications* (1986).

Campagna, Daniel S. and Donald L. Poffenberger, *The Sexual Trafficking in Children*. Dover, MA: Auburn House (1988).

Davis, Laura, *The Courage to Heal Workbook*. New York: Harper and Row (1990).

de Jong, Allan R., "The sexually abused child: A comparison of male and female victims": Comment. *Child Abuse and Neglect*, 1985, 9, 575.

Elwell, Mary E. and Paul H. Ephross, Initial reactions of sexually abused children. *Social Casework*, 1987, 68, 109-116.

Forman, Bruce D., Reported male rape. *Victimology*, 1982, 7, 235-236.

Forward, Susan with Craig Buck, *Toxic Parents*. New York: Bantam (1989).

Freeman-Longo, Robert E., The impact of sexual victimization on males. *Child Abuse and Neglect*, 1986, 10, 411-414.

Freud, Anna, *Normality and Pathology in Childhood*. New York: International Universities Press (1965).

Frosh, Stephen, No man's land? The role of men working with sexually abused children. *British Journal of Guidance and Counselling*, 1988, 16, 1-10.

Gannon, J. Patrick, *Soul Survivors: A New Beginning for Adults Abused as Children*. New York: Prentice Hall Press (1989).

Hite, Shere, *The Hite report on Male Sexuality*. New York: Alfred A. Knopf (1981).

Gil, Eliana, *Outgrowing the Pain: A Book for and about Adults Abused as Children*. San Francisco: Launch Press (1984).

Howard, Judith A., Societal influences on attribution: Blaming some victims more than others. *Journal of Personality and Social Psychology*, 1984, 47, 494-505.

Hunter, Rosemary S., Nancy Kilstrom, and Frank Loda, Sexually abused children: Identifying masked presentations in a medical setting. *Child Abuse and Neglect*, 1985, 9, 17-25.

Janus, Mark-David, Ann W. Burgess, and Arlene McCormack, Histories of sexual abuse in adolescent male runaways. *Adolescence*, 1987, 22, 405-417.

Johnson, Robert L. and Diane Shrier, Past sexual victimization by females of male patients in an adolescent medicine clinic population. *American Journal of Psychiatry*, 1987, 144, 650-652.

Johnson, Robert L. and Diane K. Shrier, Sexual victimization of boys: Experience at an adolescent medicine clinic. *Journal of Adolescent Health Care*, 1985, 6, 372-376.

Keitt, Ruth M. and Mary A. Wagner, Brian - a team approach to helping an abused child. *Elementary School Guidance and Counseling*, 1985, 20, 136-140.

LaCalle, Trula Michaels, *Voices*. New York: Berkley Books (1987).

Lew, Mike, *Victims No Longer*. New York: Nevraumont (1988).

Masson, Jeffrey Moussaieff, *The Assault on Truth*. Penguin Books (1985).

McCormack, Arlene, Mark-David Janus, and Ann W. Burgess, Runaway youths and sexual victimization: Gender differences in an adolescent runaway population. *Child Abuse and Neglect*, 1986, 10, 387-395.

Mc Govern, Kevin B. and Cathy Mc Govern, *Alice Doesn't Babysit Anymore*. Portland, OR: McGovern and Mulbacker Books (1985).

Middelton-Moz, Jane, *Children of Trauma: Rediscovering your discarded self*. Deerfield Beach, FL: Health Communications, Inc. (1989).

Miller, Alice, *For Your Own Good: Hidden Cruelty in Child-rearing and the Roots of Violence*. New York: Farrar, Strauss, Giroux (1983).

Miller, Alice, *The Drama of the Gifted Child: How Narcissistic Parents Form and Deform the Emotional Lives of Their Talented Children*. New York: Basic Books (1981).

Miller, Alice, *Thou Shalt Not Be Aware: Society's Betrayal of the Child*. New York: New American Library (1986).

Murphy, Wiiliam D., Mary R. Haynes, Susan J. Stalgaitis, and Barry Flanagan, Differential sexual responding among four groups of sexual offenders against children. *Journal of Psychopathology and Behavioral Assessment*, 1986, 8, 339-353.

Nielsen, Terryann, Sexual abuse of boys: Current perspectives. *Personnal and Guidance Journal*, 1983, 62, 139-142.

Porter, Eugene, *Treating the Young Male Victim of Sexual Assault*. Syracuse: Safer Society Press (1986).

Reinhart, Michael, Sexually abused boys. *Child Abuse and Neglect*, 1987, 11, 229-235.

Risin, Leslie I. and Mary P. Koss, The sexual abuse of boys: Prevalence and descriptive characteristics of childhood victimizations. *Journal of Interpersonal Violence*, 1987, 2, 309-323.

Rosenthal, James A., Patterns of reported child abuse and neglect. *Child Abuse and Neglect*, 1988, 12, 263-271.

Sebold, John, Indicators of child sexual abuse in males. *Social Casework*, 1987, 68, 75-80.

Segal, Zindel and William Marshall, Discrepancies between self-efficacy predictions and actual performance in a population of rapists and child molesters. *Cognitive Therapy and Research*, 1986, 10, 363-375.

Spada, James, The Spada Report. New York: The New American Library (1979).

Swift, Carolyn, The prevention of sexual child abuse: Focus on the perpetrator. *Journal of Clinical Child Psychology*, 1979, 8, 133-136.

Swift, Carolyn, Sexual victimization of children: An urban mental health center survey. *Victimology*, 1977, 2, 322-327.

W., Kathleen and Jewell E., *With Gentleness, Humor and Love: A 12-step guide for adult children in recovery*. Deerfield Beach, FL: Health Communications, Inc. (1989).

Waterman, Caroline and Deborah Foss-Goodman, Child molesting: Variables relating to attribution of fault to victims, offenders, and nonparticipating parents. *Journal of Sex Research*, 1984, 20, 329-349.

Whitfield, Charles L., *Healing the Child Within*. Deerfield Beach, FL: Health Communications, Inc. (1987).